DISCOVERING AMERICA'S FIRE MUSEUMS

Compiled and Edited by
W. Fred Conway

Library of Congress Cataloging in Publication Data
Conway, W. Fred

Discovering America's Fire Museums
Library of Congress Catalog Number: 93-090053

FBH Publishers, P.O. Box 711, New Albany, IN 47151-0711
© W. Fred Conway

Although the publisher has made a diligent effort to insure accuracy, in a compilation of this nature and scope, inaccuracies are inevitable. The publisher accepts no responsibility for any loss or inconvenience attributed to the information in this book. Museum curators and administrators are urged to submit corrections, additions, photographs, etc. for use in subsequent editions.

All rights reserved. No part of this publication may be reproduced, stored in a retrieval system, or transmitted in any graphic, mechanical, photocopying, recording, or otherwise without the prior written permission of the author and the publisher.
Printed in the United States of America

Front Cover Picture: 1875 Clapp and Jones fifth size steam fire engine. New York State Museum, Albany, NY

Back Cover Picture: Annual Steam Day at the Fire Museum of Maryland, Lutherville, MD

Typography and Layout: Pam Jones

Cover Design: Ron Grunder

THE AMERICAN FIREMAN
"Rushing to the Conflict"

Currier & Ives 1858

THE AMERICAN FIREMAN
"Prompt to the Rescue"

Currier & Ives 1858

A Fireman's Prayer

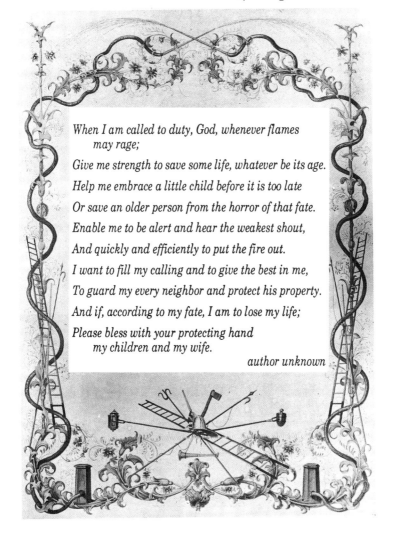

When I am called to duty, God, whenever flames may rage;

Give me strength to save some life, whatever be its age.

Help me embrace a little child before it is too late

Or save an older person from the horror of that fate.

Enable me to be alert and hear the weakest shout,

And quickly and efficiently to put the fire out.

I want to fill my calling and to give the best in me,

To guard my every neighbor and protect his property.

And if, according to my fate, I am to lose my life;

Please bless with your protecting hand my children and my wife.

author unknown

ACKNOWLEDGEMENTS

The editor wishes to thank the many curators and administrators of the nation's fire museums for their splendid cooperation in supplying the information and pictures used in this guidebook. Special thanks go to the International Association of Fire Chiefs (IAFC) for their cooperation in supplying much additional information, and to David Lewis, Curator of the Aurora Regional Fire Museum in Aurora, Illinois for his encouragement and access to his files on many fire museums.

In a directory of this nature it is inevitable that some museums may have been inadvertently overlooked. If such is the case, please be assured it is unintentional. If you will kindly advise the publisher of any omissions or inaccuracies, they will be corrected in subsequent editions.

Over the years a highlight of my family vacations has been a visit to a fire museum. Viewing actual engines and firefighting equipment used by our forefathers is an experience to be cherished and appreciated by all who have ever fought a fire or watched a fire company in action. Our grand and noble fire service heritage is preserved for you in America's fire museums. Hopefully this guidebook will enable you to seek out and enjoy them to the fullest. They are there waiting for you, and you will be welcome!

(Ex-Chief) W. Fred Conway, Editor

CONTENTS

Foreword 9
Fire Museums of the United States
    Alabama 30
    Alaska 32
    Arizona 36
    California 38
    Colorado 50
    Connecticut 55
    Delaware 59
    District of Columbia 60
    Florida 62
    Georgia 65
    Illinois 66
    Indiana 72
    Iowa 77
    Kansas 78
    Kentucky 79
    Louisiana 80
    Maine 82
    Maryland 84
    Massachusetts 90
    Michigan 100
    Minnesota 104
    Mississippi 108
    Missouri 110
    Montana 111
    Nebraska 112
    Nevada 115
    New Hampshire 120
    New Jersey 122
    New York 128
    North Carolina 141
    Ohio 143
    Oklahoma 150
    Oregon 152
    Pennsylvania 154
    Rhode Island, South Carolina, South Dakota 165
    Texas 166
    Virginia 172
    Washington 176
    Wisconsin 178
Fire Museums of Canada 182

FOREWORD

Visiting one of the 150 or so museums in the United States displaying vintage firefighting apparatus, equipment, and memorabilia is a fascinating experience for all ages. The cry of "FIRE!" conjures up the sights, sounds, and smells of a battle between man and fire, the demon that will spread and utterly destroy everything in its path if it is not controlled and extinguished. The crackling of flames, the smell of smoke, the sounds of sirens, bells, and roaring engines responding and pumping make our hearts beat faster and our adrenalin flow.

But fighting fires in times past was a far cry from firefighting today. When American colonies were founded, the principal method of fighting fires was the simple use of buckets made from leather. Each householder was required to have a fire bucket, and at the cry of "FIRE!" the buckets were thrown into the street, where they were picked up by volunteers running to the scene of the blaze.

Two lines of citizens quickly formed to comprise the most efficient firefighting technique then in existence - the bucket brigade. Men would fill buckets with water and pass them to the next man in the line until the man

Fixed nozzle hand engine in New York City c.1733.

closest to the flames would dash the water from the bucket onto the fire. Women, and even children, would pass the empty buckets down the second line back to the water source, which was often a pond, brook, or cistern. Many fire museums have leather fire buckets on display, some of which are decorated with ornate fire scenes, along with the owner's name. They are very rare.

In the 1720's, 30's and 40's, some of the more progressive cities and towns in the colonies imported hand operated fire engines from England, which were known as "hand tubs" simply because they were essentially a tub on wheels to which was affixed a piston pump with handles to be worked up and down in the manner of a railroad handcar. These first imported engines were very small, and could be pumped by two or four men. The nozzle, mounted on top of the engine, was in a fixed position, and to move the stream of water the entire engine had to be turned.

Next came a "gooseneck" nozzle, which could be adjusted without changing the position of the engine. These early hand engines were kept filled by the ever faithful bucket brigades.

Improved hand tub engine with gooseneck nozzle.

In the early 1800's fire hose was invented, which was made of leather and was held together with copper rivets. Although primitive by today's standards, it worked! And in the mid 1700's yankee ingenuity began to produce hand engines made in the colonies which soon surpassed in efficiency their English counterparts. Many of America's fire museums exhibit early hand tub engines as well as riveted leather fire hose.

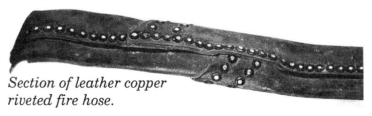

Section of leather copper riveted fire hose.

Hand engines reigned as the backbone of America's firefighting arsenal for nearly a century, and during that time many large ones were built requiring as many as forty or even sixty men to operate a single fire engine at full capacity. And, they were able to draft or suck up water through a suction hose dropped into a pond or cistern right into the engine, thus eliminating the bucket brigades.

Large hand engine requiring up to 24 men to operate.

When the fire was too far from the water source, the water was pumped from engine to engine in a relay operation. At the peak of the hand engine era in the mid 1800's, the most powerful ones could pump as much as 300 gallons per minute - a far cry from the bucket brigades of the previous century, but still primitive by today's standards. Although hand engines were used in America's villages well into the 1900's, a new invention in the mid 1800's led to their demise. The new invention used steam. A single steam fire engine with several men could do the work of six hand engines each using dozens of men!

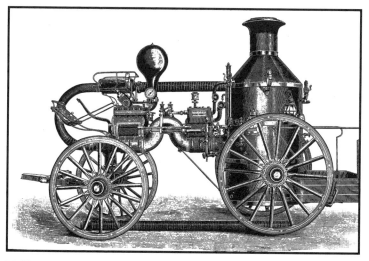

Village size steam fire engine.

The first successful steam fire engine was made in Cincinnati in 1852, with the last one manufactured in 1914, but during that half century steam fire engines became the new backbone of America's firefighting arsenal. Instead of manpower to operate the fire pumps, steam did the job so efficiently that in large cities paid firemen replaced the volunteers.

The steam fire engines, weighing as much as four tons, were pulled to fires by horses, which were well trained and loved by the firemen. There were several sizes of "steamers" ranging from the village size which pumped 300 gallons per minute to the "double extra first size" for large cities which could pump up to 1,200 gallons per minute. Many fire museums feature one or more steam fire engines.

Three horses were required to pull the larger size steamers.

In 1870 a Frenchman, Dr. F. Carlier of Paris, invented a new type of fire engine which seemed at first to have the potential for eliminating the new steamers. In fact, his invention of the "chemical engine" did extinguish some 80% of all fires for half a century - from 1872 to 1922, - but its use was limited to small fires. The chemical engines mixed soda water and acid in their tank after they arrived at a fire to create instant carbon dioxide gas under pressure to force the water out of the tank through

Double tank chemical engine, horse drawn.

a small hose and nozzle. These engines were eminently successful since they required only seconds to go into action, and they often snuffed out small fires before the arrival of the cumbersome steamers. The very first chemical fire engine exported to the United States by Dr. Carlier is pictured on page 74 and is on display at an Indiana fire museum. It became the prototype for thousands of similar engines manufactured in America by Babcock, Holloway, and others. But for large fires the steamer was supreme until the first decade of the 1900's when yet another new invention - the gasoline powered internal combustion engine - proved even more efficient than the steamers, and they could propel the engines to fires, replacing the firemen's beloved horses.

During the transition from steamers to motorized fire pumps, gasoline powered two wheeled tractors often pulled the steamers to fires instead of horses. The huge investment cities had in their steamers could not be wasted. But by the 1920's the transition to motorized fire trucks was almost complete.

Motorized "triple combination" apparatus included a fire pump, chemical tank, and a hose bed for 2-1/2" hose.

Most of the early trucks were "triple combinations" meaning that they had a fire pump, a chemical tank for small fires, and a hose bed full of 2-1/2 inch diameter fire hose. In previous years the hose had been carried on hand drawn or horse drawn reels and carts. The motorized fire trucks even carried ladders, enabling them to often do the job previously requiring four separate pieces of equipment - the steam pumper, the chemical engine, the hose reel, and the ladder wagon. Of course, for tall buildings ladder trucks were still required, as they are today.

Many of today's powerful fire trucks, which are powered by diesel engines, pump as much as 2,000 gallons per minute and carry a vast array of tools and equipment to cope with virtually any type of fire or rescue situation.

A favorite type of motorized fire truck displayed at many fire museums is the Ahrens Fox pumper, which has a large piston fire pump mounted on the front of the engine with a distinctive chrome plated

Ahrens-Fox engine with piston pump and spherical air chamber mounted in front of the motor.

ball or sphere, which is an air chamber to even out the flow of water and minimize the pulsation of the pistons. Used by many of America's larger cities, they were considered to be the most rugged and reliable pumpers that money could buy. But many other manufacturers, with American LaFrance and Seagrave being the largest, produced fire apparatus of equal power and dependability. Today all large fire pumps are of the contrifugal type rather than the piston and rotary pumps often used several decades ago.

In addition to featuring fire apparatus, many of America's fire museums display tools, accessories, accouterments, articles of dress, and other memorabilia associated with fire service history from colonial times to the present. Although the following items are not intended to comprise an all-inclusive list, they represent many of the items you will see in fire museums across America.

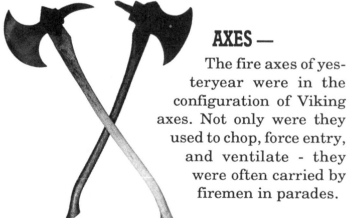

AXES —

The fire axes of yesteryear were in the configuration of Viking axes. Not only were they used to chop, force entry, and ventilate - they were often carried by firemen in parades.

TRUMPETS —

Not musical instruments, the fire officer's trumpet was a megaphone through which he shouted orders to the men at the scene of a fire. Ornate silver or nickle plated engraved trumpets were a popular gift for retiring fire chiefs and were called "presentation trumpets."

BED KEYS —

The most prized possessions of colonists were often their beds, and the metal bed frames could be quickly disassembled with a small wrench known as a "bed key," which each volunteer fire company carried. The bed was often carried out in pieces from a burning house.

TORCHES —

Before the advent of electricity, a runner, often a boy, would run ahead of the hand engine at night, holding a torch to light the way. Sometimes torches were fitted onto the engines themselves. Fancy "presentation torches" were another popular gift for retiring fire officers.

LANTERNS —

First whale oil and then kerosene lanterns were used for illumination by firemen before electric lanterns came in to use during the 1920's. Every piece of fire apparatus carried lanterns, and "presentation lanterns" engraved with the chief's name and fire department motif were another popular retirement or anniversary gift.

WOODEN WATER MAINS —

On display in various fire museums are cross sections of early (1700's) water mains made from hollowed out logs. When firemen needed water from a nearby main they would drill a hole in the log, and then stop up the hole with a plug after the fire was out. Thus a fire hydrant is still today often referred to as a "fire plug."

HATS, CAPES & PARADE BELTS —

For parades and social functions, early firemen wore stove pipe hats with the name and number of their fire company. Some had eagles or fire scenes painted on them as well. The dress uniform was often a colorful cape worn over the shoulders, and a wide leather belt with the fire company's name was also standard.

DISCOVERING AMERICA'S FIRE MUSEUMS

FIRE EXTINGUISHERS & GRENADES —

Soda-acid extinguishers, mostly 2-1/2 gallons in capacity, were carried on virtually all fire apparatus beginning in the 1870's. Other types of extinguishers included those utilizing carbon tetrachloride and dry powder comprised mainly of bicarbonate of soda, as well as foam. Special extinguishers called "fire grenades" were made of glass and were hurled at the flames, where they would shatter, with their liquid contents vaporizing into heavier-than-air fumes to smother the fire by depriving it of oxygen. They were very popular for a time, but of questionable value.

BADGES —

Firemen's badges were works of art which included fancy designs incorporating eagles, ladders, axes, hydrants, etc. as well as the name, number, and title of the fire company and fireman. Many badges are on display in fire museums.

HELMETS —

Early helmets were made of hard leather and had high front pieces. Most fire museums have early fire helmets on display. The long curving brim at the back of the helmets served to keep water and plaster from going down the fireman's neck.

The most famous volunteer fireman of them all — Benjamin Franklin, is shown wearing his traditional fire helmet with high front piece.

FIRE MARKS —

Sometimes fire insurance companies paid volunteer fire companies for extinguishing fires in insured properties. Extra payments sometimes went to the companies arriving first. To identify the properties they had insured, fire insurance companies attached a metal sign to the front of the house or building, and these fire marks have become rare collectors' items.

SLIDING POLES —

Around 1850 the firemen's brass sliding pole was invented, enabling firemen in the second floor bunk room of the fire house to get to the apparatus floor faster than using the stairs when an alarm came in. Several fire museums have a functional sliding pole as an exhibit.

FIRE ALARM INSTRUMENTS — Watchman's Rattles —

The earliest fire alarms, other than yelling "FIRE!" included a wooden rattle - a ratchet noisemaker device which was twirled by a night watchman to arouse the sleeping citizenry; and the ringing of church bells. But in 1852 telegraphy was introduced in Boston and shortly thereafter in other cities to summon firemen.

Fire Alarm Boxes —

Fire alarm boxes were located on street corners. They activated loud electro-mechanical gongs in fire headquarters or in the engine houses themselves. The gongs tapped out the number of the fire alarm box, and by counting the strokes, the firemen knew where to respond. Fire alarm equipment on display in many fire museums includes street boxes, gongs, indicators, transmitters, repeaters, registers, and take-up reels, the use of which is demonstrated and explained by museum personnel.

GONG & INDICATOR COMBINED

When an alarm was transmitted the number of the box would appear in the windows, and the gong would bang out the number as well.

In addition to exhibits of fire apparatus and fire related artifacts, some fire museums offer programs on fire prevention and fire safety. Why not take this directory along with you on every vacation and seek out one or more fire museums in the area you are visiting. A much greater appreciation of our noble fire service heritage awaits you at America's fire museums!

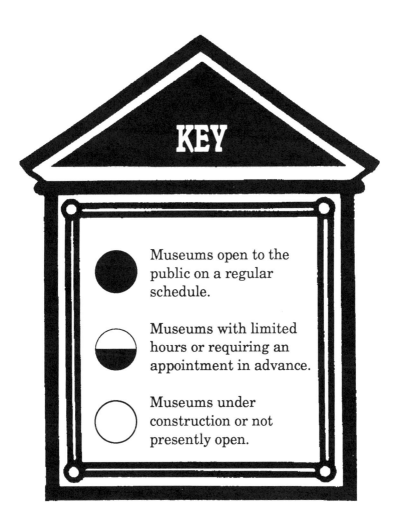

DISCOVERING AMERICA'S FIRE MUSEUMS

ALABAMA
MOBILE

● **Phoenix Fire Museum**
203 S. Claiborne Street
just off I-10 near downtown Mobile

In the American scene, few sights have ever rivaled, for thrill and drama, the flashy old steam fire engines. With the stacks belching a black fury of smoke, with the clanging of their bells and the twin eager strain of horses and men charging forward, they have left vivid memories of an unforgettable era.

The Phoenix Fire Museum occupies the home station house of the Phoenix Steam Fire Company No. 6, which was organized in 1838. The handsome building, erected in 1859, was completely restored for use as a museum in 1964 and dedicated by the wife of U.S. President Lyndon B. Johnson.

The collections housed in the museum pertain to the history of firefighting in Mobile since 1819, when the first volunteer companies were organized.

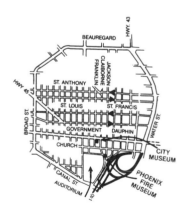

Exhibits: Hose carts, two steam fire engines, 1917 American LaFrance hook and ladder, badges, leather buckets, helmets, and other memorabilia.

Schedule:
Tues. - Sat.:
    10:00 a.m.-5:00 p.m.
Sun.: 1:00 p.m.-5:00 p.m.

Admission: Free

Phone: (205) 434-7620

DISCOVERING AMERICA'S FIRE MUSEUMS

ALABAMA
Phoenix Fire Museum

DISCOVERING AMERICA'S FIRE MUSEUMS

ALASKA
VALDEZ

● Valdez Heritage Center

This 1907 restored Ahrens steamer is one of several pieces of fire apparatus on display. It remained in service until 1935.

Exhibits: This museum also displays many aspects of the Alaska Gold Rush and the earthquake which destroyed the city in 1964. Valdez is the terminus of the trans-Alaska oil pipeline.

Schedule:
Open daily mid-May to mid-Sept.
Open Tues. - Sat. mid-Sept. to mid-May.

Admission:
Free, but donations are welcome. $1.00 per adult suggested.

DISCOVERING AMERICA'S FIRE MUSEUMS

ALASKA
WASILLA

● **Museum of Alaska Transportation and Industry**
Parks Highway Mile 46.7

Exhibits: Six pieces of fire apparatus as well as a good display of fire service memorabilia. Other displays include farm implements, railroad cars, antique automobiles, and fishing vessels. Picnic area and playground.

This 1921 American LaFrance engine pumped non-stop for 13 days in 1922 at a mine fire at Jonesville, Alaska. It has been completely restored.

Schedule:
Mon. - Sat. year round except Decoration Day and Memorial Day
8:00 a.m.-4:00 p.m.

Admission:
Adult: $3.00
Student: $1.50
Family: $7.00

Phone:
(907) 376-1211

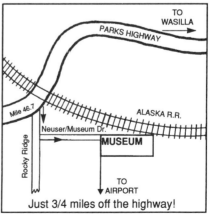

Just 3/4 miles off the highway!

DISCOVERING AMERICA'S FIRE MUSEUMS

ALASKA
Museum of Alaska Transportation & Industry

AMERICAN-LaFRANCE

- *Shatters All Known Pumping Records* -

Thirteen Days' Continuous Pumping in Zero Weather Adds a New Chapter to the Accomplishments of

American-LaFrance Motor Fire Apparatus

O N November 23rd, 1922, a serious mine fire was discovered at Jonesville, Alaska. To fight the fire a Type 12 American-La France Pumper was summoned from the Anchorage, Alaska, fire department.

It was thirteen days before the fire was extinguished. *During that time the American-LaFrance pumper worked continuously* with the exception of brief stops at irregular intervals for the purpose of changing the oil, and replacing hose that had blown couplings.

To make this performance all the more remarkable, the thermometer at the time of the fire was hovering around the zero mark.

Two hundred pounds pump pressure was maintained, which is equivalent to driving the car 9400 miles at top speed practically without interruption.

Engineering principles evolved from 80 years' experience in building fire apparatus, selection of the best materials, the thorough testing of every car we produce, and superior manufacturing methods, combine to make unusual performances typical of American-La France Motor-Driven Fire Apparatus.

Note: This American LaFrance advertisement concerns the engine illustrated on the previous page.

DISCOVERING AMERICA'S FIRE MUSEUMS

Volunteer Fireman
and
President
of the United States

George Washington

DISCOVERING AMERICA'S FIRE MUSEUMS

ARIZONA
PHOENIX

● **Hall of Flame**
6101 East Van Buren
located in the
Phoenix Activity Complex

The Hall of Flame is considered to be the largest and most comprehensive fire museum in the world.

At left is an 1870 Parade Carriage, one of over 100 pieces of fire apparatus.

Exhibits: Over 100 wheeled pieces, operating fire alarm systems, hundreds of pictorial objects, firemarks, arm patches, library of 4,000 volumes, and much more. Over 30,000 square feet of exhibit galleries. All vintage apparatus is beautifully restored. For fire buffs, this museum is a "must visit," and is the standard by which all fire museums are measured.

Schedule: Mon. - Sat., 9:00 a.m.-5:00 p.m.
Closed Thanksgiving, Christmas, New Years Day

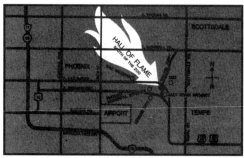

Admission:
Adults: $4.00
Sr. Citizens: $3.00
Students: $1.50
Under age 6: Free

Phone:
(602) "ASK-FIRE"

DISCOVERING AMERICA'S FIRE MUSEUMS

ARIZONA
Hall of Flame

Hand-drawn engine c. 1900.

This side-stroke hand engine is a veteran of the Great Chicago Fire of 1871.

DISCOVERING AMERICA'S FIRE MUSEUMS

CALIFORNIA
BENECIA

◖ Benecia Fire Museum
160 Military West

Exhibits:
In addition to the engines pictured is a 1884 Rumsey hand engine, photographs, badges, ribbons, trophies, old extinguishers including grenades.

Schedule:
First and third Sundays of each month from Noon to 5:00 p.m. or by appointment.

Admission:
Free. Donations appreciated.

Phone:
(707) 745-1688

1855 Hunneman hand engine.

DISCOVERING AMERICA'S FIRE MUSEUMS

CALIFORNIA
Benecia Fire Museum

1820 "Philadelphia style" double decker hand engine was originally built for New York City and came to Benica in 1850 to protect the docks.

CALIFORNIA
LONG BEACH

◯ Long Beach Firemen's Museum
1445 Peterson Avenue

Described as "a fire buff's paradise," this museum has ten wheeled pieces including the 1890 Rumsey hand-drawn ladder wagon and the 1922 Ahrens Fox pumper shown below.

Exhibits: Other apparatus includes two early hose carts, 1890 Hugo Maher hand engine, 1894 Amoskeg steamer, 1894 horse-drawn Robinson hose wagon, 1923 Seagrave aerial, 1935 GMC Squad, 1926 Ahrens-Fox pumper. There are pumping demonstrations.

Schedule:
Second Saturday of each month from 10:00a.m.-3:00 p.m.

Admission:
Free

CALIFORNIA

LOS ANGELES

◒ County of Los Angeles Fire Museum
1320 N. Eastern Ave. at Fire Dept. Headquarters

Exhibits: 1853 Button hand engine, 1903 Metropolitan steamer (pictured below), 1923 Ford TT chemical, 1925 Stutz engine, 1931 Seagrave aerial, 1938 Seagrave engine, 1957 Crown, 1973 Dodge "Squad 51" from the television show "Emergency!" Also photographs, helmets, badges, alarms, and more.

Schedule: Open weekdays by request.

Phone: (805) 267-2411

Manufactured in 1903 by the American Fire Engine Co., this Metropolitan steamer pumps 700 gallons per minute. It served in Sacramento on front-line duty until 1920, and in reserve status until 1924, when it was sold to Fox Studios, where it was featured in the film "Gone With The Wind."

DISCOVERING AMERICA'S FIRE MUSEUMS

CALIFORNIA
LOS ANGELES

● Old Plaza Firehouse
134 Plaza Street

This museum in downtown Los Angeles houses a restored horse-drawn chemical engine. Below are a side view and front view of the engine. Note the horse collars.

Schedule: Open weekdays from 10:00 a.m.-5:00 p.m.

DISCOVERING AMERICA'S FIRE MUSEUMS

CALIFORNIA
LOS ANGELES

● Travel Town
5200 Zoo Drive near Forest Lawn Exit of the Ventura Freeway at the northwest corner of Griffin Park

"Firefighting in Los Angeles: 1869-1940" is the theme of this museum, which includes the 1910 Anderson hook and ladder truck pulled by a 1913 Seagrave tractor pictured below.

Exhibits: Other wheeled pieces include a Hayes aerial truck, 1923 Seagrave pumper, 1918 American LaFrance ladder truck and a 1937 American LaFrance triple combination pumper. Also exhibited at this museum are trains, streetcars, aircraft, and vintage automobiles.

Schedule: Open daily 9:00 a.m.-5:00 p.m.

Admission: Free

Phone: (213) 662-5874

DISCOVERING AMERICA'S FIRE MUSEUMS

CALIFORNIA
SAN DIEGO

● **The Firehouse Museum**
1572 Columbia Street

Exhibits: 7 motorized rigs (1914-1942), 1903 ALF steamer, 3 hand pumpers, hand-drawn chemical rig and hose reels, extinguishers, leather buckets, helmets, badges, bells, shoulder patches, miniature apparatus, and much more.

Schedule: Thurs. - Sun., 10:00 a.m.-4:00 p.m.

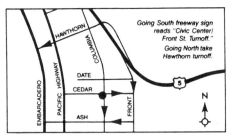

Admission:
Free. Donations welcome.

Phone:
(619) 232-3473

DISCOVERING AMERICA'S FIRE MUSEUMS

CALIFORNIA
The Firehouse Museum

Bringing the exciting history of fire fighting to life.

45

DISCOVERING AMERICA'S FIRE MUSEUMS

CALIFORNIA
SAN FRANCISCO

● **San Francisco Fire Department Museum**
Presidio Avenue between Bush and Pine Streets

*Side stroke hand tub c. 1810 –
one of San Francisco's first fire engines.*

Exhibits: One of the largest displays of firefighting apparatus, artifacts and memorabilia in the west. 1909 Gortner water cannon, restored 1937 tank wagon, nozzles, leather buckets, trumpets, helmets, lanterns, exhibit of the great fire of 1906, and much more.

Schedule:
Thurs. - Sun., 1:00 p.m.-4:00 p.m.

Phone:
(415) 861-800, ext. 365

DISCOVERING AMERICA'S FIRE MUSEUMS

CALIFORNIA
San Francisco Fire Department Museum

DISCOVERING AMERICA'S FIRE MUSEUMS

CALIFORNIA

STOCKTON

● **Pioneer Museum & Haggin Galleries**
Pershing Avenue at Rose Street

Exhibits: Three antique fire engines: an 1853 piano box style hand engine, an 1862 Neafie & Levy second-class steamer, and an 1873 Babcock chemical.

Schedule: Open daily except Mondays and holidays from 1:30 p.m.-5:00 p.m.

Admission: Free

SUNNYVALE

◐ **Ahrens Fox Fire Buff's Association**

Exhibits: Various Ahrens Fox pumpers plus collection of Ahrens Fox memorabilia.

Schedule: By appointment only.

Phone: (408) 735-7188

Volunteer Fireman and President of the United States

Thomas Jefferson

DISCOVERING AMERICA'S FIRE MUSEUMS

COLORADO
DENVER

● **Denver Firefighters Museum**
1321 Tremont Place

HOSE REEL, 1875. Pulled by volunteer firemen.

Exhibits: Two American LaFrance engines from the 1920's, leather helmets, trumpets, uniforms, trophies, fire records, alarm boards, photographs, 1867 hand pumper, sliding poles.

Special Feature: Old Number One Firehouse Restaurant with a menu of 12 different lunch choices.

Schedule: Mon.-Fri., 11:00 a.m.-2:00 p.m.

Admission:
Adults: $2.00
Children: $1.00

Phone: (303) 892-1436

*On the National Register of Historic Places.
One block from the U.S. Mint.*

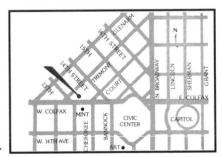

DISCOVERING AMERICA'S FIRE MUSEUMS

COLORADO
Denver Firefighters Museum

This 1867 hand pumper was pulled across the plains by oxen from Cincinnati to Denver.

DISCOVERING AMERICA'S FIRE MUSEUMS

COLORADO
PUEBLO

● Hose Co. No. 3 Museum
116 Broadway

Housed in an 1881 fire station, this regional fire museum features one of the most beautiful vintage hose carts left in the United States. The bright hickory wood, brass and steel cart dates back to 1850. In addition to the pumper pictured below there are two Ford Model T chief's cars dated 1921.

Exhibits: Memorabilia includes helmets, lanterns, buckets, nozzles, toy fire engines, trumpets, extinguishers, fire alarm equipment, tools, and much more.

Schedule: Mon.-Fri., 10:00 a.m.-2:00 p.m.

Admission: By donation.

Phone: (719) 544-4548

1917 restored American LaFrance pumper.

COLORADO

LOVELAND
● **Antique Firehouse**
3312 North Garfield Avenue

Exhibits: Apparatus on exhibit includes the following pumpers: 1916, 1920, 1922, 1929, 1950 American LaFrance; 1925, 1926, 1941 Seagrave, 1941 Ford; and a 1923 Boyer chemical engine.

Schedule: Mon.-Sat., 9:00 a.m.-5:00 p.m.

Phone: (303) 667-7040

Volunteer Fireman and American Patriot

Benjamin Franklin

DISCOVERING AMERICA'S FIRE MUSEUMS

CONNECTICUT
EAST WINDSOR

● **Connecticut Fire Museum**
I-91 Exit 45 on Route 140

1927 Mack "Bull Dog"

Also known as the Trolley Museum Fire Department, this museum features more than 18 wheeled pieces of fire apparatus from 1894-1955. There is an 1894 fire sleigh, and motorized pumpers by American LaFrance, Seagrave, Ahrens-Fox, Mack, Maxim, Peter Pirsch, GMC, Reo, and Zabek. There is a collection of fire truck models, alarm equipment, and other memorabilia.

Schedule:
April, May, Sept., Oct.:
  Sat. & Sun, Noon-5:00 p.m.
June, July, Aug:
  Mon-Fri., 10:00 a.m.-4:00 p.m.
  Sat., 10:00 a.m.-5:00 p.m
  Sun., Noon-5:00 p.m.

Admission: Nominal

Phone: (203) 623-4732

DISCOVERING AMERICA'S FIRE MUSEUMS

CONNECTICUT
MANCHESTER

● **Connecticut Firemen's Historical Society**
230 Pine Street

Exhibits: A varied collection of hand-pulled hose reels, engines, chemical engines, early motorized engines, leather fire buckets, and colorful displays of tools, badges, and lanterns. There is a steam pumper and a magnificently decorated four wheel hand-pulled hose reel. Wooden water main, watchman's rattle, bells, trumpets, and a rare fire warden's staff.

Schedule:
Fri. - Sat.: 10:00 a.m.-5:00 p.m., Sun.: Noon-5:00 p.m. from mid-Apr. through mid-Nov.

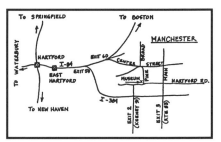

Admission:
By donation.

Located at 230 Pine Street, Manchester, Connecticut, at the intersection with Hartford Road. It can be reached from Exit 59 off I-84 by driving east on I-384 taking Exit 2 or Exit 3 (Route 83) to Hartford Road and Pine Street.

DISCOVERING AMERICA'S FIRE MUSEUMS

CONNECTICUT
Connecticut Firemen's Historical Society

A century ago, apparatus was used for fighting fires and parades. This hand-pulled hose reel only drew cheers in the line of march!

You'll see the past come alive with leather fire buckets, a fire axe and an old "fireman" weathervane.

This ornate, beautifully carved walnut chair saw long service at firehouse meetings in the late 19th century.

57

CONNECTICUT

BETHEL
◒ **Bethel Historical Firefighters Museum**

Exhibits: 1815 hand-drawn engine, Badger chemical cart, hose reels, 1936 Mack Junior, patches, badges, nozzles, helmets, toys, alarm boxes.

Schedule: By appointment only.

Phone: (203) 794-8523 or (203) 743-3825

STONINGTON
● **Cannon Square Fire Museum**
3 High Street, Stonington Town Dock

Gift Shop.

Exhibits: Houses the private collection of Timothy G. Stillman.

Schedule: Open Memorial Day through Labor Day, 10:00 a.m.-4:00 p.m. Other times by appointment.

Phone: (203) 535-3471

WINDSOR LOCKS
● **Windsor Locks Historical Museum**
11 Ahern Avenue

Exhibits: Includes a 1936 American LaFrance "Scout" pumper, which is housed in an all-brick barn built in 1826.

Schedule:
Open April through October.
Other times by appointment.

DISCOVERING AMERICA'S FIRE MUSEUMS

DELAWARE
WILMINGTON

◒ **Wilmington Fire Department Museum**
300 North Walnut Street

DISCOVERING AMERICA'S FIRE MUSEUMS

DISTRICT OF COLUMBIA

● **District of Columbia Fire Safety Education Center and Museum**
438 Massachusetts Avenue, N.W.

A National Historical Landmark.

Exhibits: Horse-drawn steamers, motorized apparatus, collections of buttons and badges. Housed in the former home of Metropolitan Hook & Ladder Co. No. 1.

Admission: Free

◐ **Friendship Fire Association Museum**
4930 Connecticut Avenue, N.W.
Located on the second floor of Engine 31/Rescue Squad 4

Exhibits: Leather fire buckets, helmets, belts, trumpets, badges from all 50 states and various foreign countries.

Schedule: Open by appointment only.

Phone: (301) 229-5290

● **National Museum of American History**
14th Street and Constitution Avenue

Exhibits: Includes five vehicles.

Schedule:
Open April 1 - Labor Day from 10:00 a.m.-7:00 p.m.
Winter Schedule: 10:00 a.m.-5:30 p.m.

Admission: Free

Phone: (202) 357-2025

DISCOVERING AMERICA'S FIRE MUSEUMS
DISTRICT OF COLUMBIA

● **Smithsonian Institution**
14 Street and Constitution Avenue N.W.

Exhibits: This huge museum includes a significant collection of antique fire apparatus, including the "Alert" hand pumper built in Salem, Massachusetts in 1840.

Schedule: Open April through August from 9:00 a.m.-10:00 p.m.

Admission: Free

George Washington fighting a fire.

FLORIDA
JACKSONVILLE

● **Jacksonville Fire Museum**
12 Catherine Street

1806 Hand Engine

Exhibits: Housed in old fire station No. 3, this museum includes, in addition to the apparatus pictured, a fire alarm box system, antique fire extinguishers, fire marks, photographs, fire department ledger books, old ladders, and much more.

Schedule:
Mon.-Fri., 9:00 a.m.-5:00 p.m.

Phone:
(904) 633-3473

DISCOVERING AMERICA'S FIRE MUSEUMS

FLORIDA
Jacksonville Fire Museum

1898 American LaFrance steamer.

1926 American LaFrance pumper.

FLORIDA

LARGO
○ **National Kid's Fire Museum**
13094 95th Street, North

Exhibits: Not yet open at press time, this museum is in the planning stages, and will feature nine operational antique fire engines. The museum is a project of the Missing Children's Awareness Foundation.

Phone: (813) 585-5360

ORLANDO
● **Fire Station No. 3 Museum**
812 East Rollins Street

Exhibits: A "Metropolitan" steamer and a 1915 American LaFrance Model 12 motorized engine. Also a superb collection of extinguishers, nozzles, badges, atlas life net, 1885 hose cart with buckets, and other memorabilia.

Schedule: Open Tuesday - Friday, 9:00 a.m.-5:00 p.m. and Saturday - Sunday, Noon-5:00 p.m.

Admission: Adults: $2.00
Seniors: $1.50
Children: $1.00

POMPANO BEACH
● **Pompano Beach Fire Museum**

Exhibits: Apparatus includes 1926 and 1948 American LaFrance pumpers, plus many artifacts, antique toys, 1926 log books, helmets, uniforms, and photographs spanning 60 years.

Phone: (305) 786-4348

GEORGIA

ROSWELL

● **Roswell Fire Museum**
1002 Alpharetta Street
in the Central Fire Station

Exhibits: Include hand tools, models of early equipment, photographs, and descriptions of memorable fires.

Admission: Free

Phone: (404) 641-3730

WOODBINE

◐ **Woodbine International Fire Museum**
2nd Street and Bedell Avenue

Exhibits: Three-wheeled chemical extinguishers, helmets, nozzles, lanterns, buckets, toy fire engines, patches, tools, grenades, and much more.

Schedule: Open daily year round.

Admission: Free, but donations appreciated.

DISCOVERING AMERICA'S FIRE MUSEUMS

ILLINOIS
AURORA

◯ **Aurora Regional Fire Museum**
Corner of New York and Broadway
(Route 25)

Exhibits: Housed in an 1895 fire station, this new museum includes early horse stalls, an alarm room, and hose tower. Apparatus includes an 1850's hand engine, a 1916 Jeffries/Pirsh engine, a 1921 Stutz/Pirsch, and a 1942 American LaFrance. Artifacts include a life net, leather hose, and souvenirs from the Great Chicago Fire of 1871. There are also many uniforms and photographs.

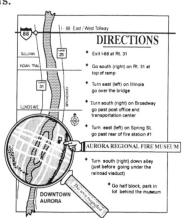

Schedule:
May thru October
  Sat. 1:00 p.m.-4:00 p.m.

Nov. thru April
  Chance or appointment.

Phone: (708) 892-1572

DISCOVERING AMERICA'S FIRE MUSEUMS

ILLINOIS
Aurora Regional Fire Museum

Early smoke mask - one fireman turns the crank on the air pump, which sends fresh air through a rubber hose to the fireman wearing the mask.

ILLINOIS
ELGIN

○ **Elgin Fire Barn No. 5 Museum**
533 St. Charles Street

This new fire museum is scheduled to open during late 1993, and at press time the operating schedule had not yet been established. It is housed in a 1904 firehouse listed on the National Register of Historic Places, with the original ornamental hay mow and brass sliding pole.

Exhibits: Apparatus includes an 1869 Silsby steamer, a 1929 American LaFrance pumper, and a 1954 Ward LaFrance pumper. There is an extensive collection of helmets, uniforms, nozzles, buckets, badges, and an operational Gamewell fire alarm board with pull boxes, repeater, gongs, indicators, and registers.

DISCOVERING AMERICA'S FIRE MUSEUMS

ILLINOIS
Elgin Fire Barn No. 5 Museum

1869 Silsby third class steamer.

1954 Ward LaFrance pumper.

ILLINOIS

CHICAGO

- **Chicago Historical Society Museum**
  North Avenue and Clark Street

  Exhibits: This museum features a gallery of fire service relics, including a display of artifacts from the Great Chicago Fire of 1871.

MENDOTA

- **Time Was Village Museum**
  1325 Burlington Road

  Exhibits: This museum complex consists of nine buildings, one of which is a firehouse containing equipment, helmets, trumpets, and other memorabilia. There are four pieces of both hand-drawn and motorized apparatus.

  Phone: (815) 539-6042

VOLUNTEER FIREMAN
AND
AMERICAN PATRIOT

John Hancock

DISCOVERING AMERICA'S FIRE MUSEUMS

INDIANA
FORT WAYNE

- **Firefighters' Museum**
  226 West Washington Blvd.

Exhibits: 1848 Button "piano box" hand engine, 1893 Amoskeag extra first size steamer rated at 1100 G.P.M., 1927 Ahrens-Fox 750 G.P.M. pumper, and eight more motorized pieces dating from 1929-1955. Also a complete alarm room, fire safety maze, films on fire prevention, artifacts and memorabilia.

Special Feature:
Museum Cafe

Schedule:
Mon.-Fri.,
11:00 a.m.-2:00 p.m.

Admission:
Adults: $1.00, Children: $.75

Phone: (219) 426-0051

DISCOVERING AMERICA'S FIRE MUSEUMS

INDIANA
Firefighters' Museum

DISCOVERING AMERICA'S FIRE MUSEUMS

INDIANA
NEW ALBANY

● **Conway Fire Museum**
4115 Profit Court, New Albany Industrial Park North

The first chemical fire engine in the United States, sent over from Paris, France by the inventor of the soda-acid principal for extinguishing fires. This engine was the prototype for every chemical fire engine in America.

Coming into the Louisville area from the north, south, or east, follow the map to I-65 Exit 6 and take I-265 west to the Grant Line Road Exit. Turn right on Grant Line Road 500 feet to Hausfeldt Lane. Turn left on Hausfeldt Lane and go one mile. Turn right on Earnings Way. We're the fourth building on the right.

Coming in from the west, take I-64 Exit 121 onto I-265 to the Grant Line Road Exit. Turn left on Grant Line Road and go 1/4 mile to Hausfeldt Lane. Go left on Hausfeldt for one mile to Earnings Way. We're the fourth building on the right.

INDIANA

Conway Fire Museum

Exhibits: Five hand-drawn and one motorized engine, hose cart, fire alarm telegraph instruments, extinguishers, buckets, trumpets, sliding pole, other memorabilia from the lifetime collection of ex-chief W. Fred Conway.

Schedule:
Mon.-Fri., 9:00 a.m.-5:00 p.m.
Saturdays by appointment.

Admission: Free

Phone: (812) 945-2617

1922 Ford Model T American LaFrance chemical.

1855 Button Squirrel Tail Piano Box Engine.

INDIANA
TERRE HAUTE
- **Historical Fire Station No. 9**
  1728 South Eigth Street

  Exhibits: Displays of both fire and police equipment.

  Schedule: First Sunday in May through first Sunday in October.

  Phone: (812) 235-9865

DISCOVERING AMERICA'S FIRE MUSEUMS

IOWA

MASON CITY
● **Van Horn's Antique Truck Museum**
Highway 65 North

1920 GMC chemical truck.

Exhibits: Fifty trucks from 1909 through 1929, including fire trucks, one of which is a Reo one cylinder. Also brass lamps, lanterns, and antiques.

Schedule: May 25-September 22, Monday - Saturday, 10.30 a.m.-4:00 p.m.. Sunday 11:00 a.m.-6:00 p.m. Other times by appointment.

Phone: (515) 423-0550

Located just North of Mason City, Iowa on Hwy. 65.

When traveling on I-80, take I-35 at Des Moines, we are 135 miles North. When traveling on I-90, take I-35 at Albert Lea, we are 35 miles South, our location is just 8 miles East off I-35. An easy way is to take County Road B-20 off I-35 just North of Clear Lake and go 8 miles East to Hwy. 65 and then one mile to your left.

KANSAS
See Kansas City, Missouri

DISCOVERING AMERICA'S FIRE MUSEUMS

KENTUCKY
LOUISVILLE

● The Filson Club Museum
1310 South Third Street

Exhibits: Hand pumper "Veteran" c. 1850. Built by William Jeffers Co. of Pawtucket, R.I., displayed in an exquisite setting in the Filson Club Museum. This beautifully restored Philadelphia-style engine is thought to have been originally used by the city of New Albany, Indiana, across the Ohio River from Louisville.

Schedule:
Mon.-Fri., 10:00 a.m.-4:00 p.m. Closed on national holidays.

Admission: Free. Donations accepted.

Phone: (502) 635-5083

✽ *Also see Indiana, New Albany, which is part of the Louisville, Kentucky metropolitan area.*

DISCOVERING AMERICA'S FIRE MUSEUMS

LOUISIANA
GRETNA

◔ Louisiana State Fire Museum
205 Lafayette Street

The single item on exhibit is the 1876 steamer built by the B.S. Nichols & Co. of Burlington, VT, which was purchased for $3,500. It was the smallest size engine built under the Gould patent, weighs 3,000 pounds, and was drawn to fires by hand. It could pump 250 gallons per minute, and fought fires until about 1928.

This 1876 Nichols (Gould patent) steamer is the only one of its kind still in existence.

Schedule:
Mon.-Sat., 9:00 a.m.-4:00 p.m. or by appointment.

Admission:
Adults: $3.00
Children: $2.00

Phone:
(504) 361-3696

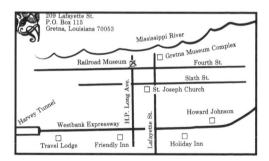

LOUISIANA

BATON ROUGE
● Baton Rouge Fire Museum
427 Laurel Street

Exhibits: Housed in the Old Bogan Central Fire Station built in 1924, this museum has the original fire pole, a 1919 ladder truck in service until 1959, a 1923 pumper, and a 1930 Model A pumper.

Schedule: The museum is shown by appointment.

Phone: (504) 344-8558

NEW ORLEANS
○ New Orleans Fire Department Museum & Educational Center
1135 Washington Avenue
in the famous Garden District

Exhibits: This new museum is scheduled to open during 1993 and will house a hand-drawn engine, hose cart and ladder wagon as well as an Ahrens steamer and 1927 Ahrens-Fox motorized pumper. Also on display will be uniforms and documents.

Phone: (504) 565-7800.

SHREVEPORT
● Shreveport Fire Fighter's Museum
830 Erie Street

Exhibits: Apparatus on display include American LaFrance: 1919, 1920, 1924, 1926, 1928, 1934 pumpers; 1928 Seagrave pumper, 1922 and 1928 Ahrens-Fox pumpers; 1942 Pirsch pumper, 1948 Mack pumper.

MAINE

OWL'S HEAD

● **Owl's Head Transportation Museum**
2 miles south of Rockland on Route 73, adjacent to Knox County Airport

Exhibits: 1896 Amoskeag steamer, 1926 Maxim pumper, 1918 Model T chemical car. Also antique autos, airplanes, tractors, etc.

Special Features: Gift shop, museum gallery, restoration workshop, energy exhibit, nature trails, picnic area.

Schedule:
May-Oct.:   10:00 a.m.-5:00 p.m., 7 days a week.
Nov.-Apr.: Weekdays, 10:00 a.m.-4:00 p.m.
            Weekends, 11:00 a.m.-3:00 p.m.

Phone: (207) 594-4418

MAINE

NORTHEAST HARBOR

● **Great Harbor Collection - The Old Firehouse**
Main Street

Exhibits: 1927 American LaFrance ladder truck, 1850 Hunneman hand engine, daily living artifacts from the 18th and early 19th centuries.

Schedule: June - October, 10:00 a.m.-5:00 p.m.

Admission: Free

PORTLAND

◓ **City of Portland Fire Museum**
In an old firehouse with three horse stalls.

Exhibits: Hand pumper used in 1866 fire, two other hand tub engines, 1938 McCann pumper built in Portland, postcards, badges.

Schedule: June 1 - September 1
Saturdays, 2:00 p.m.-5:00 p.m.,
Mondays, 6:00 p.m.-9:00 p.m.

MARYLAND
HEBRON

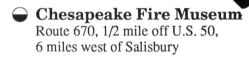

◯ **Chesapeake Fire Museum**
Route 670, 1/2 mile off U.S. 50,
6 miles west of Salisbury

Exhibits: This new 8,000 square foot museum houses 20 pieces of hand-drawn, horse-drawn, and motorized fire apparatus, including 1890 and 1908 steamers, and apparatus made by American LaFrance, Seagrave, Mack and Crown.

Other exhibits include helmets, lanterns, buckets, nozzles, toy fire engines, trumpets, extinguishers, uniforms, badges, patches, tools, appliances, slide pole, and much more.

Schedule: Open by appointment.
Admission: Free
Phone: (410) 749-3255 or (410) 546-3117

DISCOVERING AMERICA'S FIRE MUSEUMS

MARYLAND
Chesapeake Fire Museum

One of the uniform cases containing vintage dress uniforms.

Items pictured include a fireboat deluge gun and 1880 hand engine.

MARYLAND

LUTHERVILLE

◯ Fire Museum of Maryland
1301 York Road

Although operating with limited hours, this 18,000 square foot fire museum is one of the most comprehensive in America.

1850 Rodgers hand engine

Exhibits: Almost 60 pieces of fire apparatus dating from 1822 to 1957. Engines are in operating condition. The largest working fire alarm telegraph display in America is a feature.

Movies are shown in the theater. Additional exhibits include badges, uniforms, tools, pictures, banners, models, trumpets, hats, helmets, and much more.

Schedule: May-Oct., Sundays, 1:00 p.m.-5:00 p.m.
Other times by appointment.

Admission:
Family - maximum: $8.00
Adults: $3.00
Firefighters and
   Senior Citizens: $2.00
Children under 12: $1.00
Under 4: Free

Phone: (410) 321-7500

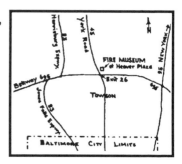

The Museum is located behind the Heaver Plaza Office Building, just one block North of Exit 26 (Lutherville) of the Baltimore Beltway (I-695).

DISCOVERING AMERICA'S FIRE MUSEUMS

MARYLAND
Fire Museum of Maryland

New York pedestal alarm box station surrounded by typical turn-of-the-century horse-drawn apparatus.

DISCOVERING AMERICA'S FIRE MUSEUMS

MARYLAND

BALTIMORE

● **Fire Museum of the Baltimore Equitable Society**
21 North Eutaw Street

Exhibits: Visitors can pump an engine, ring a firebell, sound a watchman's rattle, or try on a helmet or parade hat. Exhibits include an 1805 hose reel, uniforms, torches, lanterns, rattles, extinguishers, hand engine, helmets, fire marks, parade hats, trumpets, buckets.

Schedule: Monday - Friday, 9:00 a.m.-4:00 p.m. Closed weekends and holidays.

Admission: Free

◐ **Baltimore City Fire Museum**
Gay and Ensor Streets

Located in an old firehouse built in 1853 which includes a tower for a night watchman who scanned the skyline for signs of fire. The tower is 117 feet tall.

Schedule:
Open every weekend year round.
Other times by appointment.

VOLUNTEER FIREMAN
AND
AMERICAN PATRIOT

Samuel Adams

DISCOVERING AMERICA'S FIRE MUSEUMS

MASSACHUSETTS
BEDFORD

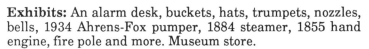

● **New Bedford Fire Museum**
Bedford and South Sixth Street

Exhibits: An alarm desk, buckets, hats, trumpets, nozzles, bells, 1934 Ahrens-Fox pumper, 1884 steamer, 1855 hand engine, fire pole and more. Museum store.

Admission: Nominal admission charge.

Colorful display of vintage uniforms.

Schedule: Open daily from 11:00 a.m.-3:00 p.m.

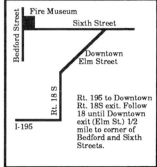

Rt. 195 to Downtown Rt. 18S exit. Follow 18 until Downtown exit (Elm St.) 1/2 mile to corner of Bedford and Sixth Streets.

DISCOVERING AMERICA'S FIRE MUSEUMS

MASSACHUSETTS
New Bedford Fire Museum

*Display of speaking trumpets
including presentation trumpets.*

DISCOVERING AMERICA'S FIRE MUSEUMS

MASSACHUSETTS
BREWSTER

● **New England Fire & History Museum**
Cranberry Highway, Route 6A

Exhibits: On display is a magnificent collection of more than 30 hand-drawn and horse-drawn fire apparatus. Guides describe where and how they were used. Fire bells ring, lights flash, and imaginations run wild.

In addition to the engines there are displays of old-time helmets (including those of fire buff Arthur Fiedler), trumpets, a rare 1929 Mercedes motorized engine, fire history movies, and thousands of items. Gift shop, picnic area.

Schedule:
Memorial Day- Mid Sept.
　Daily: 10:00 a.m.-4:00 p.m.
　Weekends: Noon-4:00 p.m.
Mid-Sept. -
　Columbus Day Weekend
　Weekends only
　10:00 a.m.-3:00 p.m.

Admission: Yes.
Children 5-12: reduced rates.
Children 4 and under: Free

Phone: (508) 896-571
Winter: (508) 945-9413

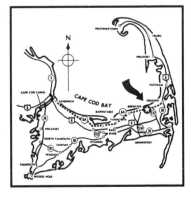

DISCOVERING AMERICA'S FIRE MUSEUMS

MASSACHUSETTS
New England Fire & History Museum

MASSACHUSETTS
HINGHAM

◯ **Bare Cove Fire Museum**
Cove Park off Fort Hill Street

1935 Ahrens-Fox pumper.

The complete record of firefighting in Hingham as displayed at this museum offers the opportunity to learn how firefighting developed in cities and towns all across America. An extraordinary collection of artifacts, equipment and documents alongside restored antique fire apparatus tell the story.

The museum's collection includes more than a dozen hand-drawn, horse-drawn, and motorized pieces, as well as leather buckets, badges, playpipes, helmets, tools, and over 600 photographs.

Schedule: Contact the Museum for regular hours.

Phone: (617) 749-0028

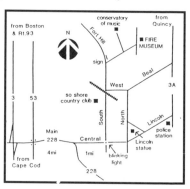

DISCOVERING AMERICA'S FIRE MUSEUMS

MASSACHUSETTS
Bare Cove Fire Museum

1922 Maxim Service Ladder & Chemical Truck.

DISCOVERING AMERICA'S FIRE MUSEUMS

MASSACHUSETTS
NEWBURY

● American Hand Fire Engine Society Museum
Zero Morgan Avenue

This is the only fire museum in America devoted entirely to hand-drawn engines. Engines illustrated: "Franklin H. Reed" was built by Hunneman in 1845, "Protection No. 1" was built by Jeffers in 1865, and "Edwin R. Lay" was built by Jeffers in 1866.

Also on display are an 1850's hose reel, hand engine models, muster trophies dating back to the mid-1800s, badges, ribbons, prints, and artifacts, all from the hand engine era.

Schedule: Shown by appointment.

Phone: (508) 465-3948 or (508) 462-7063

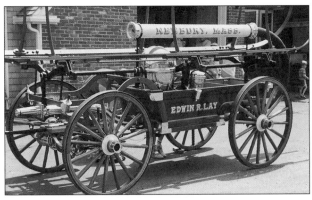

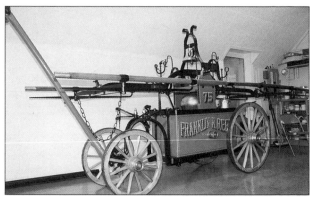

DISCOVERING AMERICA'S FIRE MUSEUMS

MASSACHUSETTS
American Hand Fire Engine Society Museum

MASSACHUSETTS

BOSTON

◐ **Boston Fire Museum**
344 Congress Street
Located in former Engine 39 and Ladder 18 quarters.

Exhibits: Two Amoskeag steamers with Christie tractors, three hand-drawn pieces, restored 1945 Ward LaFrance pumper. Also a fire alarm system, artifacts, pictures, mementos.

Schedule: View by appointment.

Phone: (617) 338-9700

BROCKTON

◐ **Brockton Fire Museum**
North Pearl Street

Schedule: View by appointment.

Phone: (508) 580-0039

NANTUCKET

● **Nantucket Historical Association**
Gardner Street

Exhibits: One of 14 museum buildings is the "Fire Hose Cart House," a descriptive exhibit of the fires at Nantucket. Another building, the "Thomas Macy Warehouse," exhibits an 1831 Cataract hand pumper, which was made in Boston. There is also a collection of fire hats, nozzles, buckets, and hose.

Schedule: During season: 10:00 a.m.-5:00 p.m. and 7:00 p.m.-10:00 p.m. daily.

Admission: Fire Hose Cart House - Free.
   Thomas Macy Warehouse - $4.00
   All 14 buildings - Adults: $8.00, Children: $4.00.

MASSACHUSETTS

PITTSFIELD
◐ **Berkshire County Museum of Firefighting**
669 Perks Road

Exhibits: Apparatus consists of a steamer and a 1915 Seagrave chemical truck. Various artifacts.

SOUTH CARVER
◐ **National Fire Museum**
Route 58

Exhibits: The extensive collection of this museum includes 20 pieces of antique fire apparatus, ranging from an 1812 hand pumper to motorized pieces. The museum also contains 10 steam trains.

Schedule: View by appointment.

Phone: (617) 338-9700

SOUTH HADLEY
● **Old Firehouse Museum**
North Main Street

Exhibits: This old firehosue, constructed in 1888-89, served for 85 years and now houses firefighting memorabilia.

Schedule: May - October.

Admission: Free

DISCOVERING AMERICA'S FIRE MUSEUMS

MICHIGAN
ALLENDALE

◯ **Engine House No. 5**
6610 Lake Michigan Drive

This museum has been reconstructed from an 1880 fire house in Grand Rapids.

Pictured in front are 1928 and 1948 Ahrens-Foxes.

Exhibits: In addition to the motorized pieces pictured are 1919, 1921, and 1928 American LaFrance pumpers. Horse-drawn apparatus includes a Silsby steamer and a Babcock chemical wagon. There are two hand-drawn pieces — an 1836 Uemphraim Thayer hand engine, and an extremely rare Edward B. Leverich 1870 hose carriage in red and blue decorated with gold leaf designs.

DISCOVERING AMERICA'S FIRE MUSEUMS

MICHIGAN

HOLLAND

● **Poll Museum of Transportation**
Four miles north of U.S. 31

In addition to the 1939 Seagrave ladder truck and 1915 Ford chemical shown below, this museum features antique automobiles, bicycles, model trains, bells, toys, and military equipment. Gift shop.

Schedule: May 1 - Oct. 1, Mon. - Sat., 9:00 a.m.-5:00 p.m.

Admission: Adults: $2.00, Children: $.50.

Phone: (606) 399-1955

DISCOVERING AMERICA'S FIRE MUSEUMS

MICHIGAN

DETROIT

- **Engine House No. 11 Museum**
  Detroit Street and Grandy

  Exhibits: This museum tells the story of firefighting during Detroit's early history and depicts the progress of the fire department over the years.

  Schedule: Monday-Friday, 9:00 a.m.-5:00 p.m.

  Admission: Free.

  Phone: (313) 224-2035

GREENFIELD VILLAGE (Dearborn)

- **Henry Ford Museum & Greenfield Village**
  20900 Oakwood Boulevard

  Exhibits: Gigantic collection includes 40 pieces of fire apparatus including hand-drawn, horse-drawn, and motorized. In the village is an old hand engine house.

  Schedule: Open year round except Thanksgiving, Christmas and New Year's Day.

MUSKEGON

- **Hackley Hose Company Museum**
  510 West Clay Street

  Housed in a recreated fire station.

  Exhibits: Include hand- and horse-drawn hose carts, horse stalls with automatic harnesses, brass pole, fire alarm system, helmets, uniforms, belts, 1923 American LaFrance pumper in reserve status until 1966.

  Schedule: Mid-May through September, Wed., Sat., Sun. 1:00 p.m.-4:00 p.m.

VOLUNTEER FIREMAN AND AMERICAN PATRIOT

Paul Revere

DISCOVERING AMERICA'S FIRE MUSEUMS

MINNESOTA
MINNEAPOLIS

● **Firefighters Memorial Museum**
1100 Van Buren Street N.E.

This 20,000 square foot museum houses 15 hand- and horse-drawn apparatus, and over 25 motorized pieces. These include a 1902 Waterous hand-drawn pumper, a 1923 Ahrens-Fox pumper, a 1919 American LaFrance aerial ladder truck, an 1895 Waterous horse-drawn steamer, and an 1830 Merrick & Agnew hand tub engine.

In addition, there is a library of fire service books and publications, and collections of fire department patches, trophies, awards, fire extinguishers, fire alarm telegraph equipment and a life net.

Special features: Party room available.

Schedule: Saturdays, 9:00 a.m.-3:00 p.m. Also first Sunday of each month, 11:00 a.m.-4:00 p.m.

Admission:
Adults: $4.00,
Children: $2.00
Includes fire truck ride.

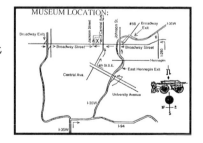

104

DISCOVERING AMERICA'S FIRE MUSEUMS

MINNESOTA
Firefighters Memorial Museum

MINNESOTA
AUSTIN
● **Austin Firefighting Museum**
Mower County Fairground

Exhibits: 1918 and 1923 motorized fire engines, two hose carts, photos of area fires, and badges from around the world.

Schedule: June - August, 9:00 a.m.-5:00 p.m.

VOLUNTEER FIREMAN AND AMERICAN PATRIOT

Alexander Hamilton

DISCOVERING AMERICA'S FIRE MUSEUMS

MISSISSIPPI
LOUISVILLE

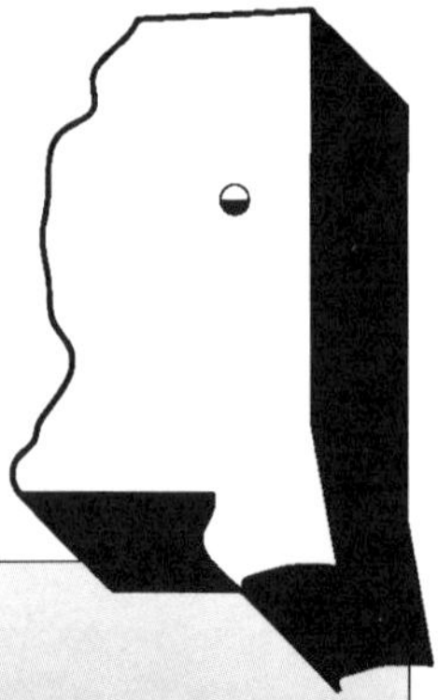

● **The American Heritage "Big Red" Fire Museum**
North Church Avenue

1924 Ahrens-Fox pumper.

Exhibits: This new and growing fire museum displays hand engines from the late 1700's, hose reels, horse-drawn ladder wagons, two steamers, 1921 city service ladder, 1924 and 1957 American LaFrance aerials, as well as the engines pictured.

In addition more than 100 fire-related artifacts are on display.

Schedule: Shown by appointment.

Admission: Free

Phone: (601) 773-3421

DISCOVERING AMERICA'S FIRE MUSEUMS

MISSISSIPPI
The American Heritage "Big Red" Fire Museum

1886 Silsby steamer.

1921 American LaFrance triple combination pumper.

DISCOVERING AMERICA'S FIRE MUSEUMS

MISSOURI

FOREST PARK
● **The History Museum**
Lindell & Debaliviere Streets in Forest Park

Exhibits: The firefighting section of this museum is called "First to the Alarm: The Story of Firefighting in St. Louis." Featured pieces are "Old Central," an 1836 hand engine, and the "Lady of the Lake" hose cart. Additional exhibits include paintings and vintage fire tools.

Schedule: Tuesday - Sunday, 9:30 a.m.-4:45 p.m.

Admission: Free

Special Feature: Handicap facilities include wheelchair ramps, elevator, handicap lift on lower level.

KANSAS CITY
◯ **Kansas City Fire Brigade Museum**
1019 Cherry

Schedule: Saturday, 9:00 a.m.-1:00 p.m.
　　　　　　Other times by appointment.

Admission: Adults: $2.00, Children: $1.00.

Phone: (816) 474-0200

ST. LOUIS
● **St. Louis Fire Museum**
1421 North Jefferson at Cass at Fire Dept. Headquarters

Exhibits: The largest fire mark collection in the midwest, helmets, axes, extinguishers, buckets, trumpets, photos, fire grenades, badges, medals, — over 700 artifacts.

Schedule: Monday - Friday, 9:00 a.m.-5:00 p.m.

Admission: Free

MONTANA

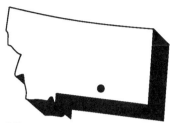

BILLINGS

● **Yellowstone County Museum**
Logan Field - Billings Municipal Airport

Exhibits: Fire equipment exhibit includes a chain fire drag used in crushing out range fires in the old west.

Schedule: Tuesday - Saturday, 10:30 a.m.-Noon and 2:00 p.m.-5:00 p.m.

Admission: Free

DISCOVERING AMERICA'S FIRE MUSEUMS

NEBRASKA
MINDEN

● **Harold Warp's Pioneer Village**
Take I-80 Exit #279

Nebraska's No. 1 tourist attraction, this museum village has over 50,000 historic items displayed in 26 buildings. Non-fire exhibits include over 350 antique autos, 100 vintage tractors, 20 flying machines, America's oldest merry-go-round, and craft demonstrations.

Exhibits: Two steamers, ladder wagon, axes, buckets, extinguishers, hand engine, trumpets, leather hose, hooks, watchman's rattle, torches, hats, 1920 Model T Ford fire truck, hose cart, lanterns, chemical cart, and various other memorabilia.

Steamer No. 17 is from Chicago, pumped 950 G.P.M. and saw service at the following fires: Iroquois Theater in 1903, Great Elevator Fire in 1908, Stockyards Fire in 1910, and the Burlington Fire in 1922.

Schedule: Open year round 7 days a week, from 8:00 a.m. to sundown.

Admission: Adults: $5.00, Children 6-15: $2.50.

Phone: 1-800-445-4447

Special Features: Motel, campground, restaurant.

NEBRASKA
Harold Warp's Pioneer Village

Note the leather fire buckets hanging on this vintage hook & ladder wagon.

1880 steamer originally horse-drawn, with a 1909 gasoline-powered front wheel drive tractor.

NEBRASKA

LINCOLN

● **Lincoln Fire Department Museum**
1801 Q Street at Fire Station #1

Exhibits: 1911 American LaFrance motorized engine, trumpet, uniforms, helmets, belts, pictures, various other memorabilia.

Schedule: Open daily 9:00 a.m.-8:00 p.m.

Phone: (402) 471-7363 or (402) 475-4558

NEVADA
LAS VEGAS

● **Imperial Palace Auto Collection**
3535 Las Vegas Boulevard South

This 2,700 room hotel and casino is home to the world-famous collection of over 200 antique, classic, and special-interest automobiles. It is located on the fifth floor of the hotel's parking facility in a plush, gallery-like setting. It includes the world's largest collection of Model J Dusenbergs.

The two engines shown, one of which is a 1913 Seagrave pumper, is part of this fabulous display.

Schedule:
Open 7 days a week, 9:30 a.m.-11:30 p.m.

Special feature: Gift shop with a wide selection of memorabilia and books.

Phone: 1-800-634-6441

DISCOVERING AMERICA'S FIRE MUSEUMS

NEVADA
RENO

● National Automobile Museum
10 Lake Street South

Exhibits: 1917 American LaFrance chemical and hose car, which was in service in Reno from 1917 until 1950! 1926 Ford TT triple combination pumper (this is the unit illustrated), 1912 Selden roadster fire chief's car modified by adding a bell, extinguishers, tool box, electric starter, and electric head lamps.

This museum also houses the most comprehensive public display of automobiles in the Western Hemisphere, with more than 200 vintage and classic cars. Over 100,000 square feet on one level.

Schedule: Open daily except Thanksgiving and Christmas, 9:30 a.m.-5:30 p.m.

Special features: Costumed interpreters, sound effects, landscaped gardens and riverside cafe, gift shop.

Admission: Adults: $7.50, Seniors: $6.50, Children ages 6-18: $2.50.

Phone: (702) 333-9300

NEVADA
VIRGINIA CITY

● Comstock Firemen's Museum
51 South C Street at Liberty Engine Co. No. 1

Exhibits: This museum exhibits original Comstock Lode firefighting apparatus and memorabilia from the early years of Virginia City, Gold Hill, and more than 50 other Nevada towns and communities. Virtually every volunteer engine, hose cart, and hook and ladder wagon ever to fight a fire on the Comstock is represented in the collection of photographs, uniforms, helmets, tools, trumpets, and hand-drawn apparatus. The collection spans the years 1861 to 1930s.

Schedule: May - October daily from 10:00 a.m.-5:00 p.m.

Admission: Free, but donations are welcome.

Two ornate hand-drawn hose reels. Note more than 30 antique fire extinguishers above the show cases.

NEVADA

CARSON CITY

- **Warren Engine Co. No. 1 Fire Museum**
111 North Curry Street

    Exhibits: This museum is located on the second floor of the fire station, and includes a massive pumper, which was the first motorized fire engine in Nevada.

VOLUNTEER FIREMAN AND AMERICAN PATRIOT

Aaron Burr

NEW HAMPSHIRE
WOLFEBORO

● **Monitor Engine Company Firehouse Museum**
South Main Street opposite Huggins Hospital

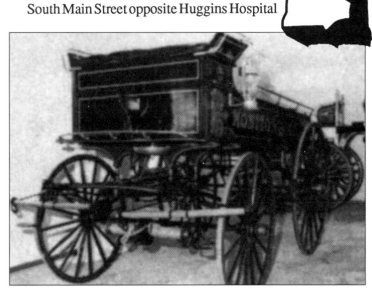

1890 Horse-drawn hose wagon.

Exhibits: Two Hunneman hand tub engines. William C. Hunneman was America's first commercial fire engine builder. He was an apprentice to Paul Revere. The Hunneman company made over 700 hand engines and two dozen steamers from 1792 to 1881. Also displayed is an 1850 two-wheel hose tender, an 1890 hose wagon, and a steamer built by the Amoskeog Manufacturing Co. of Manchester, New Hampshire. The Amoskeog Co. and its affiliated companies built 853 steamers from 1859 to 1913.

Schedule: July - Labor Day - daily except Sunday, 10:00 a.m.-4:00 p.m. or by appointment.

Admission: Free, but donations are appreciated.

DISCOVERING AMERICA'S FIRE MUSEUMS

NEW HAMPSHIRE
Monitor Engine Company Firehouse Museum

1872 Amoskeag steamer, double crane neck, second size. At 100 pounds of pressure, a hose stream reached 321 feet. This steamer was completely restored by Stephen Heaver, Jr. of the Maryland Fire Museum in Lutherville, Maryland. It represents one of the most colorful and impressive items ever manufactured in New Hampshire.

FRANKLIN
● **Franklin Firefighters Museum**
West Bow Street behind the Franklin Department

This museum, opened in 1987, features an 1853 Hunneman hand engine completely restored, with an accompanying hose reel with original riveted leather hose. Also displayed is an American steam fire engine rated at 500 G.P.M.

Exhibits: Artifacts include extinguishers, early EMS equipment, hand tools, nozzles, alarm boxes, and an electro-mechanical bell striker used to ring the box number on the church bell. On the grounds is a small hose reel house with its original hand-drawn reel.

Schedule: Open daily from Memorial Day through Columbus Day. Other times by appointment.

Admission: Free

Phone: (603) 934-2205

DISCOVERING AMERICA'S FIRE MUSEUMS

NEW JERSEY
BOONTON

● **New Jersey Firemens Museum**
565 Lathrop Avenue
at the New Jersey Firemen's Home

This splendid 8,000 square foot fire museum is housed at the 85 acre campus of the New Jersey Firemen's Home, an eight building facility for retired firemen, both paid and volunteer. Exhibits include the American LaFrance steamer pictured, a hand pumper, a 1903 Oldsmobile fire chief's car, and motorized fire engines from 1919, 1936, and 1941. Also exhibited are hundreds of fire memorabilia including leather buckets and a collection of trumpets.

Schedule: Open daily.

Admission: Free

Phone: (201) 334-0024

Directions: *From South and Central Jersey:* Garden State Parkway, Turnpike, etc., North to RT. 187 NORTH: follow signs at exit 40B to home. *Metropolitan Newark Area:* 280 West to 80 West to 287 North, then as above. *Northern New Jersey:* 80 East or West to 287 North, then as above. 202 South to 287 South, follow signs at exit 41 to Home.

DISCOVERING AMERICA'S FIRE MUSEUMS

NEW JERSEY

CAPE MAY

● Cape May Fire Museum
Washington and Franklin Streets

This quaint vintage fire station houses a 1928 American LaFrance 1000 G.P.M. pumper and other memorabilia.

Schedule: Open daily March-November. Other times check at fire station behind the museum.

DISCOVERING AMERICA'S FIRE MUSEUMS

NEW JERSEY
MILLTOWN

◖ Eureka Fire Museum
South Main Street behind the Milltown Firehouse

Exhibits: 1870 Silsby six-man hose cart, several hand-drawn hose and chemical carts, 1921 American LaFrance triple combination pumper, patches, badges, helmets, antique equipment.

Schedule: Open Monday evenings or by appointment.

Phone: (908) 828-7207 or (908) 828-0221

NEW JERSEY

BAYONNE

● **Bayonne Firefighters Museum**
111 North Curry Street

Exhibits: 1850 hand-drawn carriage, 1944 Mack pumper, photos, helmets, trumpets, fire alarm indicator and repeaters. Educational programs. National Register of Historic Buildings.

Schedule: Monday - Friday, 8:00 a.m.-3:30 p.m. Closed holidays.

Phone: (201) 858-6005

DOVER

◐ **Dover Fire Museum**
209 N. Sussex Street

Exhibits: 1812 hand engine, 1874 Rumsey hose reel, 1870's steamer, 1932 American LaFrance pumper.

Schedule: Visit by appointment.

Phone: (201) 366-0301

HOBOKEN

◐ **Hoboken Exempt Firemen's Association Museum**
201 Jefferson Street

Exhibits: An interesting collection of fire department memorabilia.

DISCOVERING AMERICA'S FIRE MUSEUMS

NEW JERSEY

NEWARK

- **Newark Fire Department Historical Association Fire Museum**
  49 Washington Street, located in the garden of the Newark Museum

  Exhibits: Several pieces of antique fire apparatus and many items of firefighting memorabilia.

  Schedule: Daily Noon - 4:30 p.m. except July 4, Thanksgiving and Christmas.

  Phone: (201) 596-6550

NEWTON

- **Newton Fire Museum**
  150 Spring Street via Rt. 80 west to Newton Rt. 206 exit.

  Schedule: Summer - open daily. Fall and winter - Fri.-Sat., 9:30 a.m.-3:30 p.m.

  Admission: Free

NORTH PLAINFIELD

- **North Plainfield Exempt Firemen's Museum**
  300 Somerset Street across from Town Hall

  Exhibits: 1800 hand pumper, 1925 hand pumper, 1842 silver hose reel, 1887 steamer, 1948 Mack pumper.

  Phone: (908) 668-8914

NEW JERSEY

PLEASANTVILLE

◐ **Firefighters Museum of Southern New Jersey**
10-12 Ryon Avenue

Exhibits: 1854 hand engine, 1929 Ahrens-Fox, 1938 Brockway, many other fire items.

SOMERVILLE

◐ **Somerville Exempt Firemen's Museum**
North Doughty Avenue in original 1888 fire house

Exhibits: 1835 hand engine, 1873 steamer, 1942 Mack pumper.

Schedule: Saturday, 10:00 a.m.-Noon.

Admission: Free

TRENTON

● **Meredith Havens Fire Museum**
244 Perry Street on third floor of Fire Dept. Headquarters

Exhibits: Extensive collection of over 3,000 items of firefighting memorabilia.

Admission: Free

Phone: (609) 883-1569 or (609) 585-0439

DISCOVERING AMERICA'S FIRE MUSEUMS

NEW YORK
ALBANY

● **New York State Museum**
Madison Ave., Empire State Plaza

At left is an ornate silver-plated hose carriage c. 1877. Non-operational, it was designed only for use in parades, and included mirrors and velvet side panels.

This museum, one of America's foremost scientific and cultural institutions, includes a dazzling display of beautifully restored vintage fire apparatus and memorabilia. Various hand-drawn, steam, and motorized pieces are featured, including an 1863 Button and Blake hand engine, a Clapp and Jones steamer, Gleason and Bailey hose cart, American steamer, 1919 American LaFrance triple combination pumper, American LaFrance water tower raised by the pressure from a chemical tank, 1938 Ahrens-Fox pumper, and many others. Other firefighting artifacts are displayed as well.

Schedule: Open daily except Thanksgiving, Christmas, New Year's Day, 10:00 a.m.-5:00 p.m.

Admission: Free

Phone: (518) 474-5877

DISCOVERING AMERICA'S FIRE MUSEUMS

NEW YORK
New York State Museum

Richard Mason Hand Tub 1791. Remained in service until 1832.

DISCOVERING AMERICA'S FIRE MUSEUMS

NEW YORK
BROCKPORT

◓ **Capen Hose Co. No. 4 Fire Museum**
at the Capen Hose Fire Station

*An 1848 Rumsey hose carriage,
one of the featured pieces of this museum.*

Exhibits: Also on exhibit is a 1930 Seagrave Suburbanite pumper named the "Grey Ghost," as well as a 1951 Seagrave custom pumper. Other displays include a working Gamewell fire alarm telegraph system, a slide pole, scaling ladder, lanterns, nozzles, firemarks, helmets, and a turn-of-the-century diorama.

Schdule: Open any time by request. Visitors are welcome and should phone ahead.

Phone: (716) 637-4713 or (716) 637-2512

Admission: Free

Volunteer Fireman
and
American Patriot

John Jay

DISCOVERING AMERICA'S FIRE MUSEUMS

NEW YORK
HUDSON

● **American Museum of Firefighting**
at the New York State Firemen's Home, just off the New York State Thruway.

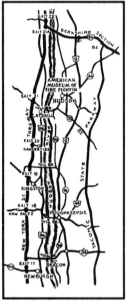

Directions: Close to NYS Thruway (Exit 21-Catskill) or Route 9W. Follow signs to Rip Van Winkle Bridge and Hudson. From the east side of Hudson River take Route 9 or Taconic State Parkway and Routes 82 and 23 to Hudson. Museum opposite middle school on Harry Howard Avenue.

Schedule: Apr.-Oct., 9:00 a.m.-4:30 p.m.

Admission: Free

NEW YORK
American Museum of Firefighting

Rumsey "Squirrel Tail" hand-drawn engine.

1928 Ahrens-Fox front-mounted 6 cyl. pumper.

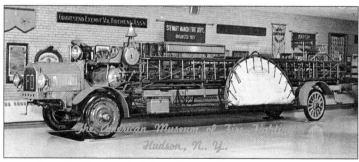

American LaFrance ladder-chemical. In service 1916-1956.

NEW YORK
MONROE

● Museum Village in Orange County
Museum Village Road

This unique village museum is contained in 48 separate buildings, one of which is the Mombasha Fire Company.

Exhibits: Fire apparatus exhibits in addition to the steamer and hand engine pictured are six more pieces including a "Washington" hand pumper, an American LaFrance metropolitan steamer, two ladder wagons, and hose carts.

Schedule: May - Dec., Sat. & Sun: Noon-5 p.m.
  Wed., Thurs. & Fri.: 10:00 a.m.-2:00 p.m.
    in July & Aug. only: 10:00 a.m.-5:00 p.m.
  Mon. & Tues.: Closed
  Open: Memorial Day,
    July Fourth and Labor Day
  Closed: Columbus Day
    & Thanksgiving

Admission: Adults: $8.00
  Senior Citizens (Age 60+): $6.00
  Children (Ages 6-15): $5.00

Phone: (914) 782-8247

DISCOVERING AMERICA'S FIRE MUSEUMS

NEW YORK
Museum Village in Orange County

1856 Side-Stroke, Craneneck Hand Engine

DISCOVERING AMERICA'S FIRE MUSEUMS

NEW YORK
NEW YORK CITY

● **The New York Fire Museum**
278 Spring Street

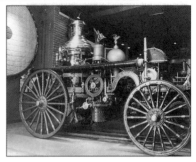

Located on Spring Street between Hudson and Varick just to the west of Manhattan's popular Soho district, The New York Fire Museum is easily accessible to visitors by public transportation – the 7th and 8th Avenue Subways have stops nearby, but routes service the area – and by automobile, through the adjacent Holland Tunnel. The building offers 13,500 square feet of usable space to effectively demonstrate the role of the firefighter in the survival and growth of New York City.

Exhibits: The Firefighting Museum of The Home Insurance Company provided a priceless and extensive view of firefighting in New York, the U.S. and the world: splendid uniforms and presentation shields; ornately decorated vehicles, some of the oldest in existence; the largest collection of insurance fire marks; as well as rare prints and documents.

The City of New York Fire Department provided an array of pumping engines, of hose trucks, of hook and ladder vehicles; many served the actual New York Fire companies still in existence today.

Schedule: Tues. - Sat., 10:00 a.m.-4:00 p.m.
Admission: Adults: $3.00, Children: $.50.
Phone: (212) 691-1303

DISCOVERING AMERICA'S FIRE MUSEUMS

NEW YORK
The New York Fire Museum

NEW YORK

BUFFALO

◒ **Buffalo Fire Historical Society**
1850 William Street at South Ogden Street

Exhibits: Includes a 1907 American LaFrance steamer, a 1960 American LaFrance tillered aerial, and show cases loaded with memorabilia and artifacts.

Schedule: Shown only by appointment. Check with Buffalo Fire Headquarters.

Phone: (201) 596-6550

CICERO

◒ **Ye Olde Fire Station Museum**
8662 Cicero-Brewerton Road (10 mi. north of Syracuse)

Exhibits: 1900 Seagrave hand-drawn four-wheel ladder wagon, 1873 Silsby steamer, 1920 Childs Model T pumper, 1925 American LaFrance 65-foot aerial ladder truck, 1921 American LaFrance pumper, 1939 Seagrave pumper, 1925 American LaFrance 65-foot aerial ladder truck. Also displays of ribbons, badges, nozzles, lanterns, uniforms, toys, alarms, extinguishers, including hand grenades.

Schedule: May 1 - November 1 daily by appointment.

Admission: Free

Phone: (315) 699-3642 or (315) 699-2761

ENDWELL

◒ **Hooper Fire Museum**
3311 East Main Street in the old Hooper School

Exhibits: Badges, ribbons, helmets, extinguishers, photographs, nozzles, buckets, fire marks, lanterns, air masks, sirens, toys, fire alarm boxes, and a hand-drawn ladder cart.

Schdeule: Shown by appointment.

Admission: Free

Phone: (607) 785-2279 or (607) 785-9175

NEW YORK

KINGSTON

● **Volunteer Firemen's Hall and Museum of Kingston**
265 Fair Street

Exhibits: Hand-drawn parade carriage, motorized apparatus, working Gamewell fire alarm telegraph system, uniforms, badges, old prints, books, documents, mugs.

Schedule: First weekend in April through last weekend in October. Friday, 11:00 a.m.-3:00 p.m. Saturday, 10:00 a.m.-4:00 p.m. Also June through August on Thursday, 11:00 a.m-3:00 p.m.

Admission: Free

Phone: (914) 331-0866 or (914) 331-4065

NEW YORK CITY

● **Museum of the City of New York**
1220 Fifth Avenue

Exhibits: Hand-drawn engine used at the Great New York Fire of December 16, 1835. Much memorabilia including prints, paintings, helmets, models.

ROCHESTER

● **Genesee Country Museum**
20 miles south of Rochester near New York Thruway Exits #47 & #46.

Exhibits: This museum consists of 50 homes, shops, and farm buildings from the 19th century in a village setting. During August there is a muster of hand-drawn and horse-drawn fire apparatus. Phone for details.

Admission: Adults: $8.00, Children: $3.50

Phone: (716) 538-2887

NEW YORK
STONY BROOK, L.I.
● **The Museum at Stony Brook**
1208 Route 25A, 1 1/2 miles west of Nichols Road
A multi-building complex.

Exhibits: Horse-drawn 1870 hose carriage, 1874 Amoskeag steam pumper.

Schedule: Wednesday - Saturday, 10:00 a.m.-5:00 p.m., and most Monday holidays. Sunday, Noon-5:00 p.m.

Admission: Free

Phone: (516) 751-0066

NORTH CAROLINA
ELIZABETH CITY

● **Museum of the Albemarle**
1116 U.S. Highway 17 South

Exhibits: Two engines including the above 1888 steamer, various equipment, trumpet.

Schedule: Tues. - Sat., 9:00 a.m.-5:00 p.m. Sun., 2:00 p.m.-5:00 p.m. Closed Monday & state holidays.

Admission: Free

Phone: (919) 335-1453

NORTH CAROLINA

CHARLOTTE

◐ **Oasis Wagoneers/Antique Fire Museum**
Oasis Shrine Temple

Exhibits: Apparatus on display includes a 1925 hook and ladder truck with a chemical tank, 1926, 1942, 1948 pumpers, 1948 city service ladder truck.

NEW BERN

◐ **New Bern Firemen's Museum**
Highway 17-70 at rear of Central Fire Station

Exhibits: 1879 Atlantic steamer in service until 1915. Various other memorabilia.

DISCOVERING AMERICA'S FIRE MUSEUMS

OHIO
CINCINNATI

● **Cincinnati Fire Museum**
315 West Court Street

Pictured is one of two Ahrens-Fox pumpers on display. Ahrens-Foxes were manufactured in Cincinnati. Note the life net in back of the engine.

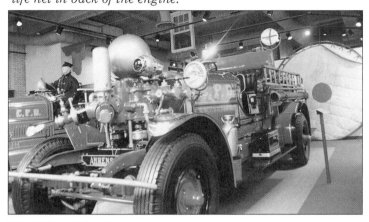

Exhibits: Also displayed is a steamer and an exquisite working model of a steamer, as well as hand-drawn apparatus. There are artifacts and memorabilia galore.

Special Features: A theater for viewing a film on early firefighting developments, a replica hand engine children can really pump, and a short slide pole children can really slide down. There is a model "Safe House" and a well-stocked gift shop.

Schedule: Weekdays, 10:00 a.m.-4:00 p.m. Weekends, Noon-4:00 p.m. Closed Mondays and holidays.

Admission: Nominal

Phone: (513) 621-5553

OHIO

NEW CARLISLE

◖ Honey Creek Fire Museum
311 North Adams Street

Exhibits: In addition to the two Rumsey hand engines pictured, there are three hose carts, a firemen's drink cart c. 1865, one 1840 cistern dump tank, trumpets, grenades, lanterns, torches, prints, tools, fire marks, rattles, helmets, axes, nozzles.

Schedule: Shown by appointment.

Admission: Free

Phone: (513) 845-0480

1870 Rumsey Hand Tub Engine.

c. 1860's Rumsey Hand Tub Engine.

DISCOVERING AMERICA'S FIRE MUSEUMS

OHIO

TOLEDO

◐ Toledo Firefighters Museum
918 Sylvania Avenue

Exhibits: Located in a 1920 fire station, this museum's million dollar display includes an 1837 hand engine that required a crew of 20 men who could pump 300 gallons per minute. Motorized pumpers: 1927 American LaFrance, 1929 Pirsch, 1935 Chevrolet, 1936 Schact service ladder truck. Also exhibited are trumpets, gongs, bells, badges, buckets, antique fire toys, watchman's desk with tape register, uniforms, scrapbooks, journals, photographs.

Special Features: Children's Fire Safety and Education Center.

Schedule: Summer: Sat., Noon-4:00 p.m. Winter: Sat. & Sun., Noon-4:00 p.m. Groups tours available weekdays or evenings by appointment.

Admission: Free

Phone: 478-FIRE

OHIO
VAN WERT

◕ Central's Fire Museum
9 Warren Road

This outstanding fire museum is housed in the headquarters of the home office of Central Insurance Companies. In addition to the 1871 hand-drawn engine and Ahrens horse-drawn steamer pictured is a 1926 Ahrens-Fox pumper as well as magnificent collections of leather buckets, 600 antique fire toys, fire extinguishers including grenades, fire marks, helmets, lanterns, engine lamps, uniforms, and much more.

Schedule: Shown by appointment.

Admission: Free

Phone: (419) 238-1010

DISCOVERING AMERICA'S FIRE MUSEUMS

OHIO
Central's Fire Museum

DISCOVERING AMERICA'S FIRE MUSEUMS

OHIO

CLEVELAND

● **Crawford Auto/Aviation Museum**
10825 East Boulevard

Exhibits: This museum houses over 200 restored vehicles, which includes steam and early motorized fire apparatus.

Phone: (216) 721-5722

COLUMBUS

● **Center of Science & Industry**
280 East Broad Street

Exhibits: This museum displays a 1930 Seagrave Suburbanite pumper in its lobby area.

Schedule: Mon. - Sat., 10:00 a.m.-5:00 p.m., Sunday, 1:00 p.m.-5:30 p.m.

Admission: Yes

Phone: (614) 228-6362

◐ **Central Ohio Fire Museum**
260 North Fourth Street

Exhibits: This museum is housed in an old two-story firehouse.

Phone: (614) 464-4099

DISCOVERING AMERICA'S FIRE MUSEUMS

OHIO

COLUMBUS
● **Nationwide Insurance Display**
North High Street and Nationwide Boulevard

This vast display of firefighting artifacts and mementos is located on the ground floor of the 40 story International Headquarters complex of the Nationwide Insurance Co.

Exhibits: 18 vintage firefighter's hats and helmets, axes, hooks, nozzles, trumpets, leather buckets, a large collection of fire marks. Scale models of horse-drawn apparatus, original Currier & Ives lithographs.

Schedule: Weekdays, 8:00 a.m.-4:30 p.m.

Admission: Free

FOSTORIA
◒ **Fostoria Area Historical Society Museum**
213 South Main Street

Exhibits: Located in the Municipal Building, this museum displays a 1937 Seagrave pumper.

MACEDONIA
◒ **Varnes' Fire Museum**
8168 South Bedford Road

Exhibits: This small museum is located in the home of Bill and Ida Varnes, but it houses over 800 toy fire engines as well as helmets, shields, patches, extinguishers, postcards, books and photographs. Also belt buckles, posters, paintings, antique pumps and fire alarms.

Schedule: Shown by appointment.

Phone: (216) 467-8783

DISCOVERING AMERICA'S FIRE MUSEUMS

OKLAHOMA
OKLAHOMA CITY

● **Oklahoma State Firefighters Museum**
2716 N.E. 50th Street, easy access from I-35 at the N.E. 50th Street Exit.

Exhibits: The original firehouse in Oklahoma territory, 1870 Hunneman hand engine, 1890 Prospect chemical cart, 1861 Amoskeag harp steamer, 1910 American LaFrance chemical & hose, 1917 American combination, LaFrance triple pumper, 1928 1920 Stutz Ahrens-Fox, 1937 Seagrave.

Also the largest known collection of shoulder patches in the world, and a mural, "The Last Alarm" on the south wall of the museum which depicts fire apparatus from the horse-drawn steamer to the mid-1950's.

Schedule: Daily, 10:00 a.m.-5:00 p.m.

DISCOVERING AMERICA'S FIRE MUSEUMS

OKLAHOMA
Oklahoma State Firefighters Museum

1907 water tower. Originally horse-drawn. Motorized tractor added in 1922. In service until 1950.

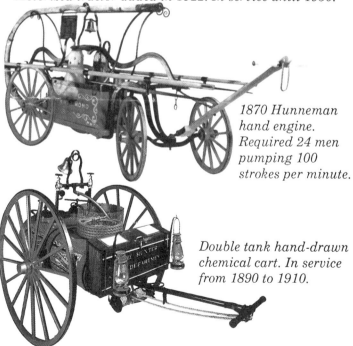

1870 Hunneman hand engine. Required 24 men pumping 100 strokes per minute.

Double tank hand-drawn chemical cart. In service from 1890 to 1910.

OREGON
PORTLAND

● **Jeff Morris Fire Museum**
55 S.W. Ash Street

The focal point of this museum, located at the Portland Bureau Headquarters is this 1911 American LaFrance horse-drawn steamer, which stayed in service until 1922 or 1923. Rediscovered in a barn in 1967, it was totally disassembled, and after two and one-half years and over 2,000 hours of work it was restored to its exact original condition, fired up, and pumped perfectly.

Exhibits: Additional exhibits include an 1863 hand engine, an 1874 Amoskeag steamer, a fire department bell mounted on a horse-drawn hose wagon, a hose cart, and miscellaneous artifacts including ladders and extinguishers.

Phone: (503) 248-0203

DISCOVERING AMERICA'S FIRE MUSEUMS

OREGON
Jeff Morris Fire Museum

DISCOVERING AMERICA'S FIRE MUSEUMS

PENNSYLVANIA
BETHLEHEM

● **The Kemerer Museum**
427 North New Street

Located in the museum annex are two vintage hand engines, one of which, "The Perseverence" is said to be the oldest fire engine in the United States, having been built in London in 1698. The "Diligence" hand tub is also on display and was imported from Neuweid on the Rhine in 1792. Other fire memorabilia is also on exhibit including helmets and trumpets.

Schedule: Open on a daily basis.

Admission: Nominal

Phone: (215) 868-6868

DISCOVERING AMERICA'S FIRE MUSEUMS

PENNSYLVANIA

DERRY

◐ **Derry Fire Museum**
Second Avenue, Route 116 East above the Derry Fire Hall

1929 American LaFrance Pumper.

Exhibits: The one-room museum is crammed full of hundreds of vintage artifacts, including helmets, extinguishers, grenades, toys, tools, and much more. Shown by appointment.

Phone: Fire Hall (412) 694-2653
Curator (412) 694-9408

DISCOVERING AMERICA'S FIRE MUSEUMS

PENNSYLVANIA

ERIE

● **Firefighters Historical Museum**
West Fifth & Chestnut Street in Old Fire Station No. 4

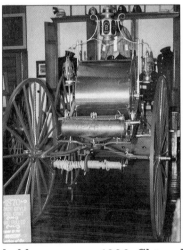

Housed in an 1873 fire station, this museum exhibits more than 1200 fire-related pieces. Perhaps the rarest of all, and the only one known to be displayed in the United States is the 1889 Remington horse-powered engine. Not only did horses pull it to the fire – they walked around it in a circle to power the pump.

Exhibits: Additional apparatus include 1823 and 1830 hand engines, 1886 and 1889 hose carts, 1888 hand-drawn ladder wagon, 1926 Chevrolet pumper, 1927 Chevrolet chemical engine, 1927 American LaFrance 1000 G.P.M. pumper, several hose carts, and various others.

Other exhibits include fire marks, badges, ribbons, extinguishers, models, helmets, uniforms, patches, working fire alarm telegraph system, 1887 tower bell, leather buckets, trumpets, and a theater for fire safety films.

Special Features: Pufferbelly Firehouse Restaurant, Gift Shop.

Schedule: May - Aug., Sat.: 10:00 a.m.-5:00 p.m., Sun.: 1:00 p.m.-5:00 p.m. Sept. - Oct., Sat. & Sun.: 1:00 p.m.-5:00 p.m. Groups by appointment.

Admission: Adults: $1.50
Senior Citizens: $1.25
Firefighters: $1.00
Children 10-16: $.50

Phone: (814) 458-5969 or (814) 864-2156

PENNSYLVANIA

Firefighters Historical Museum (Erie)

1920 American LaFrance 1000 G.P.M. pumper.

1889 Remington horse-powered fire engine – the only engine of its kind known to be on exhibit in the United States.

DISCOVERING AMERICA'S FIRE MUSEUMS

PENNSYLVANIA
PHILADELPHIA

● **CIGNA Museum and Art Collection**
17th and Arch Streets

*Foreground -
The Pioneer,
Reaney and
Neafie steam fire
engine, 1857. It is
probably the
oldest steam fire
engine in
existence.*
Background -
*1891 Silsby
steamer.
Photograph
courtesy CIGNA
Museum and Art
Collection.*

Exhibits: Wheeled pieces from the 1700's and 1800's are on display. An additional collection of fire-related artifacts from the 18th, 19th, and 20th centuries includes hand tools, fire marks, models, prints, parade capes and hats, and other paraphernalia. This collection may be viewed by advance appointment by phoning.

Schedule: Monday - Friday, 9:00 a.m.-5:00 p.m.

Phone: (215) 761-4907

DISCOVERING AMERICA'S FIRE MUSEUMS

Why are Dalmations 'Firehouse Dogs?'

Why do Dalmatians and firehouses go together like smoke and fire?

The answer is interesting, one you'll likely recall every time you see the Dalmatian/firehouse combo from now on.

It all began in the days of stagecoaches. Horse theft was so common back then that many stagecoach drivers strung a hammock between two stalls at night, then slept behind their horses to guard against thieves. But, if the driver owned a Dalmatian, he could sleep in the house or the stagecoach hotel. Why? Because it was observed that Dalmatians formed an amazingly tight bond with horses.

Since every firehouse had a set of fast horses to pull the pumper, it became common for each group of firemen to keep a Dalmatian. The spotted dogs not only guarded the firehouse horse, they kept them company during their long, boring waits between fires. And when they took off for a fire, the dog would run alongside the pumper.

The horses are gone from fire stations today, but the Dalmatians aren't. The tradition has been carried on, and it may be as much for the looks and appeal of these beautiful dogs as it is for their nostalgic tie to yesteryear.

DISCOVERING AMERICA'S FIRE MUSEUMS

PENNSYLVANIA

PHILADELPHIA

● Fireman's Hall
Second & Quarry Streets

1907 Metropolitan steamer

Exhibits: Housed in an authentic 1876 firehouse, this museum holds a priceless collection of memorabilia, graphics, film, and actual early engines and rolling stock. Hand engines and steamers are on display. The entire history of firefighting in America unfolds during a visit to this splendid fire museum, where firefighting history comes alive.

Fire marks, hand tools, and the wheelhouse of an actual fireboat are additional features. A theater shows firefighting films.

1815 hand engine

Fireman's Hall ... you wouldn't think history could be so much fun!

Schedule: Tues. - Sun., 9:00 a.m.-5:00 p.m.

Admission: Free

DISCOVERING AMERICA'S FIRE MUSEUMS

PENNSYLVANIA
Fireman's Hall

1907 Metropolitan steamer.

"Philadelphia Style" (of course) hand engine.

DISCOVERING AMERICA'S FIRE MUSEUMS

PENNSYLVANIA
YORK

◐ Fire Museum of York County
757 West Market Street

Exhibits: Motorized fire engines, with their red lights and sirens, fill the apparatus room, as if ready to answer another alarm. You can relive the experience of the early 1900's as you view a 1919 Model "T" fire engine, a 1933 Ahrens-Fox, a 1955 American LaFrance or any of our other motorized firefighting fleet. You will be able to pull a Fire Alarm Box and see and hear an original Gamewell Fire Alarm System operate as it did in the late 1800's. You will see an old-fashioned Fire Chief Office and firefighter's sleeping quarters re-created complete with brass slide pole.

Schedule: Sat.: Noon-4:00 p.m. 2nd Sunday of each month: Noon-4:00 p.m. Closed Nov. 1 to Apr. 1.

Phone: (717) 843-0464

DISCOVERING AMERICA'S FIRE MUSEUMS

PENNSYLVANIA

BOYERTON
● **Boyerton Museum of Historic Vehicles**
28 Warwick

Of the 100 vehicles on display, six are firefighting apparatus, hose carts, engine, and a ladder truck.

Schedule: Monday-Friday 8:00 a.m.-4:00 p.m.

CHAMBERSBURG
◒ **Chambersburg Volunteer Fireman's Museum**
441 Broad Street

This museum is housed in a 1906 two-story firehouse complete with brass slide pole and a Gamewell indicator.

Exhibits: 1903 LaFrance steamer, 1921 Model T Ford chemical engine, 1925 American LaFrance pumper, 1947 Mack engine painted sky blue, 1953 Oren open cab pumper, 1936 Ward LaFrance service ladder truck.

Additional exhibits include hand-drawn hose reels, ribbons, medals, helmets, uniforms.

Schedule: Spring through the end of Fire Prevention Week in October. On Saturday & Sunday from 1:00 p.m.-9:00 p.m. or by apointment.

Admission: Free

Phone: (717) 263-1049

COATESVILLE
◒ **Beaver Creek Fire Museum**
Five miles north of Coatesville and Downington

Exhibits: Fire apparatus, memorabilia, early toys, artwork.

Admission: Free

PENNSYLVANIA

HANOVER

● **Hanover Fire Museum**
201 North Franklin Street
Schedule: Daily 9:00 a.m.-8:00 p.m.
Admission: Free
Phone: (717) 637-6674

HERSHEY

● **Hershey Museum**
170 West Hersheypark Drive
Next to Hersheypark Arena

Exhibits: American LaFrance hose & ladder wagon, hand-pulled or horse-drawn, early 1900's, steamer manufactured by Button Co., hand-drawn engine dated 1812, 1805 hose cart, buckets, alarms, etc.

Schedule: Daily 10:00 a.m.-5:00 p.m. Stays open until 6:00 p.m. Memorial Day through Labor Day. Closed Thanksgiving, Christmas, New Year's Day.

Admission: Adults: $3.75, Seniors discount, Children: $1.50

Phone: (717) 534-3439

SUSQUEHANNA

◐ **Susquehanna Fire Department Museum**
410 Elm Street

Exhibits: Apparatus displayed includes an 1871 hand pumper and a 1938 Mack pumper.

Phone: (717) 853-4222 or (717) 853-4780

RHODE ISLAND
WARWICK

◐ **Greenwood Volunteer Fire Co. No. 1**
245 Morse Avenue

Exhibits: 1825 Hunneman hand tub, 1940 Mack pumper, 1954 Maxim pumper.

Phone: (401) 737-6854

SOUTH CAROLINA
CHARLESTON

◐ **Charleston Fire Dept. Museum**
262 Meeting Street in the main fire station

Exhibits: A hand engine, steamer, and 1926 Ahrens-Fox.

SOUTH DAKOTA
MURDO

◐ **Pioneer Auto Museum and Antique Town**
Junction of I-90 and Hwys. 16 & 83
Ten acres with 30 buildings of exhibits.

Exhibits: 1921 Ford Model T fire engine, 1937 Diamond T rescue truck, 1938 Diamond T fire truck. Also helmets, lanterns, buckets, nozzles, toy fire trucks, trumpets, extinguishers, tools.

Schedule: June-Aug.: 7:00 a.m.-10:00 p.m.
Apr.-May & Sept.-Dec.: 8:00 a.m.-6:00 p.m.

Admission: Adults: $4.50, Children: $2.00

Phone: (605) 669-2691

DISCOVERING AMERICA'S FIRE MUSEUMS

TEXAS
BEAUMONT

● **Fire Museum of Texas**
400 Walnut at Mulberry

Housed in the original 1927 historical Beaumont Fire Headquarters station, this museum not only has excellent exhibits, but a "Learn by Doing" Center for teaching fire prevention, a safety house, and a theater for showing fire safety films as well.

Exhibits: 1856 hand-drawn engine (pictured above), 1879 Silsby steamer, 1909 American LaFrance aerial ladder truck, 1931 searchlight truck said to be the first one ever manufactured, brass slide poles, 1901 Gamewell fire alarm system, antique fire extinguishers, leather buckets, nozzles, badges, helmets, uniforms, and much more. Fire House Gift Shop.

Schedule: Mon.-Fri, 8:00 a.m.-4:30 p.m. Closed holidays.

Admission: Free. Donations accepted.

Phone: (409) 880-3927

DISCOVERING AMERICA'S FIRE MUSEUMS

TEXAS
Fire Museum of Texas

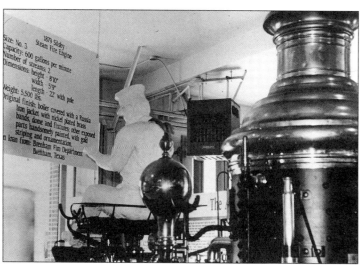

DISCOVERING AMERICA'S FIRE MUSEUMS

TEXAS
DALLAS

● **Dallas Firefighters Museum**
3801 Parry across from Fair Park in old No. 5 Fire Station

Exhibits: 1883 Ahrens steamer, 1884 hose wagon, five motorized pieces 1915-1936, helmets, lanterns, buckets, trumpets, toy fire engines, photographs, extinguishers, fire alarm office.

Schedule: Weekdays, 9:00 a.m.-4:00 p.m.

Admission: Free

Phone: (214) 821-1500

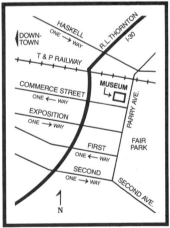

DISCOVERING AMERICA'S FIRE MUSEUMS

TEXAS
Dallas Firefighters Museum

TEXAS
HOUSTON

● **Houston Fire Museum**
2403 Milam at McIlhenny (Downtown)

Exhibits: 1884 hand-drawn engine, 1892 steamer, 1912 American LaFrance water tower (pictured at right), 1895 hand-drawn hose reel, 1923 American LaFrance pumper, 1938 Reo salvage/rescue truck. Also patches, fire marks, bells, sirens, extinguishers, helmets, uniforms, trumpets, lanterns, brass sliding pole, much more.

Schedule: Tues. - Sat., 10:00 a.m.-4:00 p.m. Sun., 1:00 p.m.-5:00 p.m.

Admission: Free

Phone: (713) 524-2526

DISCOVERING AMERICA'S FIRE MUSEUMS

TEXAS
Houston Fire Museum

*1912 American LaFrance water tower.
It was not retired from service until 1966.*

DISCOVERING AMERICA'S FIRE MUSEUMS

VIRGINIA
ALEXANDRIA

● **Friendship Firehouse**
107 South Alfred Street

The 1849 hand engine above assisted in putting out the fire at the National Capitol in 1851. It was viewed by 50 million citizens during the Bicentennial.

Schedule: Open daily.
Admission: Free

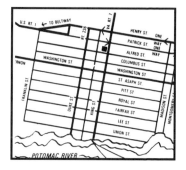

172

DISCOVERING AMERICA'S FIRE MUSEUMS

VIRGINIA
Friendship Firehouse

George Washington, a member of the Friendship Veterans Fire Engine Company, organized in 1774, purchased this engine for about $400.00 and gave it to the townspeople of Alexandria as a gift. It was transported from Philadelphia to Alexandria by ox cart. Many other artifacts are also exhibited.

VIRGINIA

MANASSAS

- **James E. Lesnick Fire Museum**
  8804 Weir Street off Route 234
  ten minutes from I-66

  Exhibits: This private collection spans three centuries and includes hose and chemical carts, thousands of fire helmets, badges, uniforms, models, photographs, rare appliances and equipment, and much more.

  Schedule: Visitors welcome evenings and weekends by appointment.

  Admission: Free

  Phone: (703) 369-5869

RICHMOND

- **Steamer Co. No. 5 Museum**
  200 West Marshall Street

  Exhibits: Highly rated by visitors from all parts of the country, this museum exhibits early hand- and horse-drawn apparatus as well as many pieces of fire memorabilia.

  Schedule: Sunday, 1:00 p.m.-5:00 p.m.. Other times by appointment.

  Phone: (804) 644-1849

Prior to 1870, Fire Alarm Boxes Were Kept Locked!

Trying to locate the key from a policeman or merchant often resulted in delayed alarms, with property destroyed and lives lost.

DISCOVERING AMERICA'S FIRE MUSEUMS

WASHINGTON
SEATTLE

○ **Last Resort Fire Department**
1433 N.W. 51st Street (contact address)

This "fire department" is made up of 22 pieces of vintage fire apparatus plus memorabilia, but as yet there is no museum building to house it.

Phone: (206) 783-4474

1927 Ahrens-Fox 1000 G.P.M. pumper.

1930 Mack 1000 G.P.M. pumper.

DISCOVERING AMERICA'S FIRE MUSEUMS

WASHINGTON
Last Resort Fire Department

1924 American LaFrance 1000 G.P.M. pumper.

1920 Seagrave 800 G.P.M. pumper.

1926 American LaFrance straight-frame tillered aerial.

DISCOVERING AMERICA'S FIRE MUSEUMS

WISCONSIN
PESHTIGO

● **Peshtigo Fire Museum**
400 Oconto Avenue

October 8, 1871 was perhaps the darkest day in fire service history in the United States. On that day the Great Chicago Fire killed 250 people, but in the small Wisconsin lumber town of Peshtigo, on that same day over 1,000 persons lost their lives in the most destructive forest fire in history – the Great Peshtigo Fire – one of the worst fire disasters of all time.

Exhibits: This fire museum, unlike other fire museums, does not display fire apparatus and firefighting artifacts. Rather, it is a memorial to the memory of the Great Peshtigo Fire and those who perished in it.

Schedule: Open daily 9:00 a.m.-5:00 p.m.

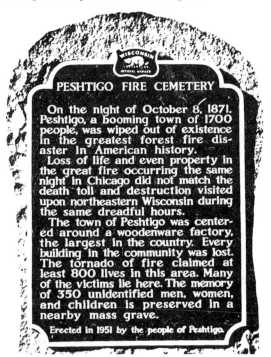

WISCONSIN

RACINE

◓ Firehouse 3 Museum
700 Sixth Street

This museum is in an old firehouse built in 1881, which was in active service until 1968.

Exhibits: The steamer illustrated below, original fire alarm telegraph equipment, brass slide pole, helmets, photographs, breathing apparatus, trophies, and other memorabilia.

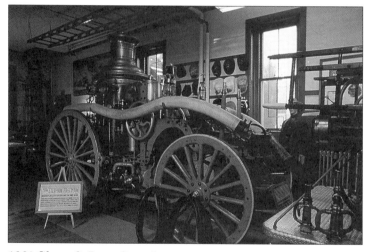

1882 Clapp & Jones first-class craneneck double pump steamer, the last of six steamers owned by the Racine Fire Department. It was in active service until 1909, but remained in service as a reserve pumper into the 1940's!

Schedule: Sunday, 1:00 p.m.-4:00 p.m. except holidays. Other times by appointment.

Admission: Free

Phone: (414) 637-7395

DISCOVERING AMERICA'S FIRE MUSEUMS

WISCONSIN

CLINTONVILLE
● **Four Wheel Drive Museum**
105 East 12th Street

Exhibits: Four wheel drive vehicles displayed include fire apparatus. Also shown are FWD race cars from the Indianapolis 500, the FWD steamer, the FWD battleship etc.

Schedule: Open daily from Memorial Day through Labor Day.

Admission: Free

MADISON
◯ **Old Fire Station #8 Museum**
407 North Street

Exhibits: This museum has three of the rigs originally housed at this station – a 1941 Pirsch quadruple combination, a 1959 FWD 1000 G.P.M. pumper, a 1959 Pirsch aerial ladder truck, and a 1956 Pirsh 1,250 G.P.M. pumper. Memorabilia on display includes life nets, helmets, coats, boots, uniforms, models, badges, axes, sliding poles, and more.

Schedule: Shown by appointment.

Phone: (608) 244-6732

MILWAUKEE
● **Milwaukee Fire Historical Society Museum**
6680 North Teutonia Avenue at the Milwaukee Fire Department Training Academy

Exhibits: Two engines, ten display cases of artifacts.

WISCONSIN

SLINGER
◐ **Historic Venerable Fire Company**

Exhibits: On exhibit are some 40 pieces of apparatus dating back to hand-drawn (1860) up through motorized pieces, which have been authentically restored. A working turn-of-the-century fire alarm system is also displayed, as are many other rare and unique items of fire service memorabila.

Schedule: First Sunday of each month May through October. 1:00 p.m.-5:00 p.m.

Phone: (414) 644-5784

STURGEON BAY
● **Door County Historical Museum**

Exhibits: Over a century of firefighting is exhibited. 1869 hand engine, 1920 Oldsmobile fire truck, 1926 W.S. Nott engine, 1939 FWD pumper. Also antique firefighting equipment and a large display of photographs of early firefighting in the area.

Schedule: May 15 through July 1, 10:00 a.m.-Noon and July 1 - September 1, 1:00 p.m.-5:00 p.m. Tues.-Sat.

Admission: Free. Donations accepted.

SUPERIOR
● **Old Firehouse and Police Museum**
Highway 1/53 - 23rd Avenue East

Exhibits: In a turn-of-the-century firehouse is a 1906 Ahrens steamer, a 1944 Mack pumper, and an early fire alarm switchboard. Also a collection of fire memorabilia. Brass sliding pole.

Schedule: June through August. Viewing by appointment during April, May, September, October.

Admission: Yes

Phone: (715) 398-7558

DISCOVERING AMERICA'S FIRE MUSEUMS

CANADA

YARMOUTH, NOVA SCOTIA

● **Firefighters Museum of Nova Scotia**
451 Main Street

This 12,800 square foot museum contains a vast collection of apparatus and memorabilia. Twenty-five pieces of rolling stock include eight hand engines by Hunneman and others, Amoskeag, Silsby, and Ronald steamers, chemical engines, hose reels, and five motorized rigs. Dates are from 1819 to 1933.

Exhibits: Helmets, lanterns, buckets, prints, books, nozzles, toy fire engines, trumpets, uniforms, fire marks, badges, patches, certificates, fire alarm equipment, tools, grenades, and more. There is a gift shop.

Schedule: Open year round. Oct.-May — Mon.-Fri., 10:00 a.m.-Noon and 2:00 pm.-4:00 p.m. July-Aug., Mon.-Sat., 9:00 a.m.-9:00 p.m. and Sunday 10:00 a.m.-5:00 p.m.

Admission: Adults: $.50, Children $.25, under age 14 - $.10.

Phone: (613) 238-6661

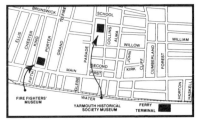

DISCOVERING AMERICA'S FIRE MUSEUMS

CANADA
Firefighters Museum of Nova Scotia

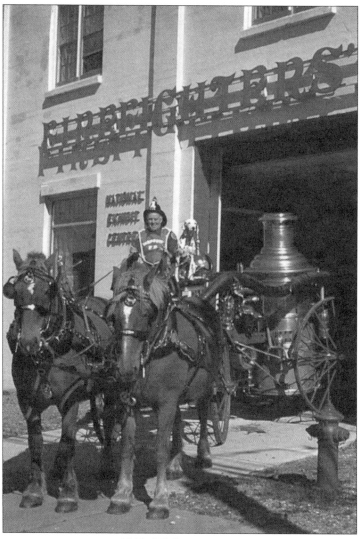

1880 Silsby steamer.

CANADA

OTTAWA, ONTARIO

● **Musee Bytown Fire Brigade Museum**
179 Clarence Street at corner of Cumberland

Exhibits: Restored antique fire trucks, working model of a fire alarm watch room, original Courier & Ives lithographs, audio-visual presentations, educational programs.

Schedule: 10:00 a.m.-5:00 p.m.

Admission: Yes, a small fee.

Phone: (613) 238-6661

MONTREAL, QUEBEC

◐ **Montreal Auxiliary Firemen Museum**
Corner of St. Lawrence Blvd. & Laurie Ave. Adjacent to Fire Station No. 30

Schedule: Open on Sunday afternoons. Other times by appointment.

Phone: Montreal Fire Headquarters

MOOSE JAW, SASKATCHEWAN

● **Western Development Museum**
Trans-Canadian Highway

Exhibits: One of the fascinating exhibits in this museum is the section of fire apparatus, which includes a hose cart, chemical wagon, chief's buggy, horse-drawn ladder wagon, steamer, a 1917 American LaFrance pumper, and a 1941 airport crash truck.

DISCOVERING AMERICA'S FIRE MUSEUMS

Other Books in the Fire Service History Series from Fire Buff House Publishers.

- **CHEMICAL FIRE ENGINES** *by W. Fred Conway*
  The only book ever written about these amazing engines that for half a century put out 80% of all fires in spite of the fact that they never did perform as advertised! Hard cover. 128 pages, over one hundred photographs and drawings.

- **FIREBOATS** *by Paul Ditzel*
  The definitive work on the history of marine firefighting - a book so real you can almost hear and feel the engines and pumps throbbing! Relive the thrilling accounts of fireboats in action at spectacular fires. Hard cover. Over a hundred pictures.

- **FIRE ALARM!** *by Paul Ditzel*
  The story of fire alarm telegraphy - a nostalgic overview of fire alarm transmission in America. Includes the incredible story of an obscure telegraph operator, John N. Gamewell, who built a vast fire alarm empire with a 90% market share. Hard cover. Hundreds of pictures.

- **LOS ANGELES FIRE DEPARTMENT** *by Paul Ditzel*
  The fascinating complete history of the Los Angeles Fire Department. America's foremost fire historian details the major fires during the city's history, including the Bel-Air brush fire disaster, and the Central library blaze. Oversize book with 250 pages and hundreds of photographs of fires and apparatus. Soft cover.

- **A FIRE CHIEF REMEMBERS**
  by Battalion Chief Edwin F. Schneider (Ret.)
  The poignant, touching, moving account of his FDNY career. Now 82 years of age, Chief Schneider looks back at the series of incredible events in his 34 year career climb from buff to chief. Soft cover. Illustrated.

- **LAGUARDIA'S FIRE CHIEF** *by Kathleen Packard Walsh*
  The fascinating biography of New York City Fire Chief/Fire Commissioner Patrick Walsh, who served under the mercurial mayor, Fiorello LaGuardia. Chief Walsh and Mayor LaGuardia would race to see who could get to the fire first. This account of Chief Walsh's storybook career is written by his granddaughter. Soft cover. Illustrated.

These books are available wherever fire books are sold, or you may order direct from the publisher.

Fire Buff House Publishers
P.O. Box 709, New Albany, IN 47151
Phone: 1-800-995-9500